Hope

the everyday and imaginary life of young people on the margins

Simon Robb, Patrick O'Leary,
Alison Mackinnon and Peter Bishop

Wakefield Press

Wakefield Press
1 The Parade West
Kent Town
South Australia 5067
www.wakefieldpress.com.au

First published 2010

Design and editing—Paul Wallace and Simon Robb.
Printed and bound by Ligare.

National Library of Australia Cataloguing-in-Publication entry

Title:	Hope: the everyday and imaginary life of young people on the margins/Simon Robb ... [et al.].
ISBN:	978 1 86254 885 5 (pbk.).
Notes:	Bibliography.
Subjects:	Young adults—South Australia—Social conditions.
	Youth—South Australia—Attitudes.
	Youth in art.
Other Authors/Contributors:	
	Robb, Simon
Dewey Number:	305.23099423

Hawke
Research Institute

The Hawke Intersections series of books aims to foster the sustainability and social justice goals of the Hawke Research Institute at the University of South Australia.

We wish to thank the Australian Research Council which funded, under its Linkage Project scheme, the University of South Australia research project 'Doing Social Sustainability: the utopian imagination of youth on the margins' (2006–08). This book stems from that project.

We would like to thank the following organisations that generously committed their resources to the research project: Youth Education Centre (Department of Education and Children's Services), Bowden Brompton Community School (DECS), Migration Museum, South Australia, Department of Further Education, Employment, Science & Technology, and the Social Inclusion Unit (Department of the Premier and Cabinet).

We would also like to thank the following people for their support: Paul Altschwager (1951–2008), Jicky Atkinson, Marina Bowshall, Bronwyn Corcoran, Anton Hart, Sam Hele, Leonie Jacka, John Leondaris, Catherine Manning, Bruce Nyland, The Hon. Stephanie Key, Jan Patterson, Peta Savage, Professor Rhonda Sharp, Trevor Short, Jeff Stotter, Viv Szerkeres, Gerri Walker and Davis Watts. Special thanks to the young people who contributed to the project.

The accounts, dialogue and images in the following pages are the thoughts and opinions of the authors and the young people who participated in the research. They do not necessarily represent the views of the organisations or people who supported the study and they are not a statement of South Australian government policy.

Ethical rules under which the research for this book was conducted required that the young people represented in the study remain anonymous. Young people contributing to this book are therefore not named and we have, for similar reasons, masked the eyes of people in their photos.

contents

author notes

Dr Simon Robb is interested in the experiences of marginalized young people and in exploring the limits of writing practice. He has published in the area of the sociology of education (Innovation and Tradition 2004) and experimental histories (The Hulk, 2003). He has also written and produced several documentaries for radio.

Patrick O'Leary PhD is Professor of Social Work Studies at the University of Southampton. Patrick's research interests are in gendered violence. He has worked on various child protection projects to support young people around the world. He has undertaken research on how people survive childhood trauma such as child sexual abuse.

Emeritus Professor Alison Mackinnon AM was Foundation Director of the Hawke Research Institute at the University of South Australia. Her research and writing spans gender and history, and issues of equity in education for girls and marginalized young people.

Peter Bishop is Associate Professor in the School of Communication, International Studies and Languages at the University of South Australia. He has researched, published and taught extensively around the topics of imagination, memory, hope, utopia and reconciliation.

preface

In 2006 a research team began a project aimed at investigating what hope and the future meant to young people on the margins of society. The research team spent time at two South Australian alternative education schools that catered for marginalised young people aged 13–18. These young people couldn't cope with mainstream schooling nor could these institutions cope with their needs. Many of the young people had major emotional, behavioural or drug problems, or engaged in criminal activities that made it impossible for them to stay within the mainstream. Their experiences were often characterised by troubled family backgrounds of violence and abuse along with involvement with child welfare. We felt that their views had been neglected. The research focused on the young people, but the teachers, social workers and related staff were also consulted. This book is the result of that research.

The research with the young people took place in their schools. At the outset the young people were invited to participate as assistant researchers on a project about hope. It was explained to them that we wanted their assistance in understanding what hope and the future might mean. We stressed that they were not the problems that the research was trying to solve, but that they were people whose understanding of hope and the future, in their own life, was valued by the researchers.

One of the planned outcomes of the research project was an exhibition entitled 'Hope' at the Migration Museum (Adelaide) in 2008. The exhibition strongly influenced the way the research was conducted. We needed methods that would lead to the production of visual, rather than simply textual, primary material that could be used in the museum. To do this we drew on research methods from visual anthropology and sociology, where photography and drawing is used to document experience and elicit information that would otherwise be inaccessible. Processes where the research subject is given the role as photographer (as sometimes occurs in the process of 'photo-elicitation') also encourages the research subject to engage creatively with the project in which they are participating.

Likewise, the autonomy and creativity offered by this method enhances the pleasure that the subject experiences during the process. Photo-elicitation was not only a research tool to 'elicit information'. It fulfilled a key need to collect objects or representations that had visual power.

The young people were given disposable cameras and asked to take photos of places, people and things that made them feel hopeful and evoked for them a sense of the future. The young people had the cameras for up to two weeks. All the students did their photography away from the research team and were free to use the cameras wherever they wanted. When the photos were developed, we returned to the school and talked with the young people about the significance of the images they had selected. All of the photos in this book, including the cover, were taken by the young people. The young people and their teachers were interviewed, sometimes individually and in sometimes in small groups, about hopefulness and the future. In keeping with the philosophy of the research, the interview technique drew on the theory that underpins narrative therapy that has a central tenet that people are not problems, problems are problems. The interviews placed young people at the centre of inquiry where both their hopes and future could be discussed and contrasted with what might be seen as a more likely future. These interviews appear in this book as first person narratives about hope and the future. The young people were also asked to draw pictures of the future, of the future that they wanted and the future that they thought was going to occur, no matter what. Those drawings also appear in this book.

Some of this material might confront the reader, assault our gentle sensibilities, but it is important for understanding the complexities of hope. While we as authors would not condone the use of a Nazi swastika, for example, or the use of violence against others, we need to consider what leads a young person to see hopefulness there—and concomitantly, to help to develop more sustainable roads to hopefulness we need to first acknowledge the presence of hope conjured up through unsustainable means.

Much of the work produced during the research process with the young people is organised into themes: people and places that make you feel hopeful, and the future. Hopefulness, according to this work, is to be found in relationships with friends and family, in caring for others and the pleasures of companionship. Yet it is also clear that sustaining these relationships may sometimes lead to violent and harmful events. Likewise, typical places of hopefulness are to found in the home, or in nature, yet hopefulness seems also to exist in any place where relationships of care and companionship can flourish, or where the self is protected or sheltered from the world outside. This might include places that appear to be ruins. We also see, in ideas about hopeful things, the presence of the car, mobile phones and the television set alongside drugs and knives. It is as if throughout this book we see the presence of mainstream hope alongside those things commonly associated with hopelessness. This is also evident in drawings about the future that display an unsettling blend of desire and destruction. How do we read these disturbing images? Are they signalling intent or trying to contain disturbing thoughts, common to many teenagers, not just those who are troubled? Or are they an expression of resistance, a desire for change or difference from the position of marginality in an attempt to break from the status quo?

As for the teachers, hopefulness is felt most strongly in relationships of openness, friendship and care that develop between themselves and the students. This was the key to discovering the hopefulness of teaching. We found that for both the young people and their teachers, hopefulness is the feeling that life is worth living or worth sustaining. This feeling can be produced through bodily experiences, relationships and the imagination. We found that hopefulness exists universally, but the way that it is produced is not necessarily benign or positive. On the one hand, hopefulness is produced in ways typically attributed to notions of social sustainability, which is through relationships of care and friendship, employment, procreation and the legal acquisition of property. On the other hand, hopefulness can also be produced by self-destructive activities and violence against others and their property; activities that are typically seen to be antithetical to a sustainable society. We would suggest that destructive activities are not the result of an absence of hope, but rather a reflection of the limited opportunities available for the production of hope through sustainable means. In the later part of the book the researchers discuss and explore the complexity and implications of some of these key themes.

The idea of researching hope and marginalised young people had its origins in a desire to expand and enrich the idea of social sustainability, which is typically about the articulation of hopes for a better society in the context of options for practical change. We decided to expand on the idea of social sustainability by thinking about hope without limits, which is another way of talking about utopias. Utopias are that aspect of hope that is left out of social sustainability. Utopias are absent from social sustainability debates, as too are the voices of those we call young people on the margins. Their views offer a different and generational challenge to the more anodyne depictions of hope and the future found in conventional views of sustainable societies, and indicate that we may need to consider the centrality of marginal ideas when thinking about hope and the future.

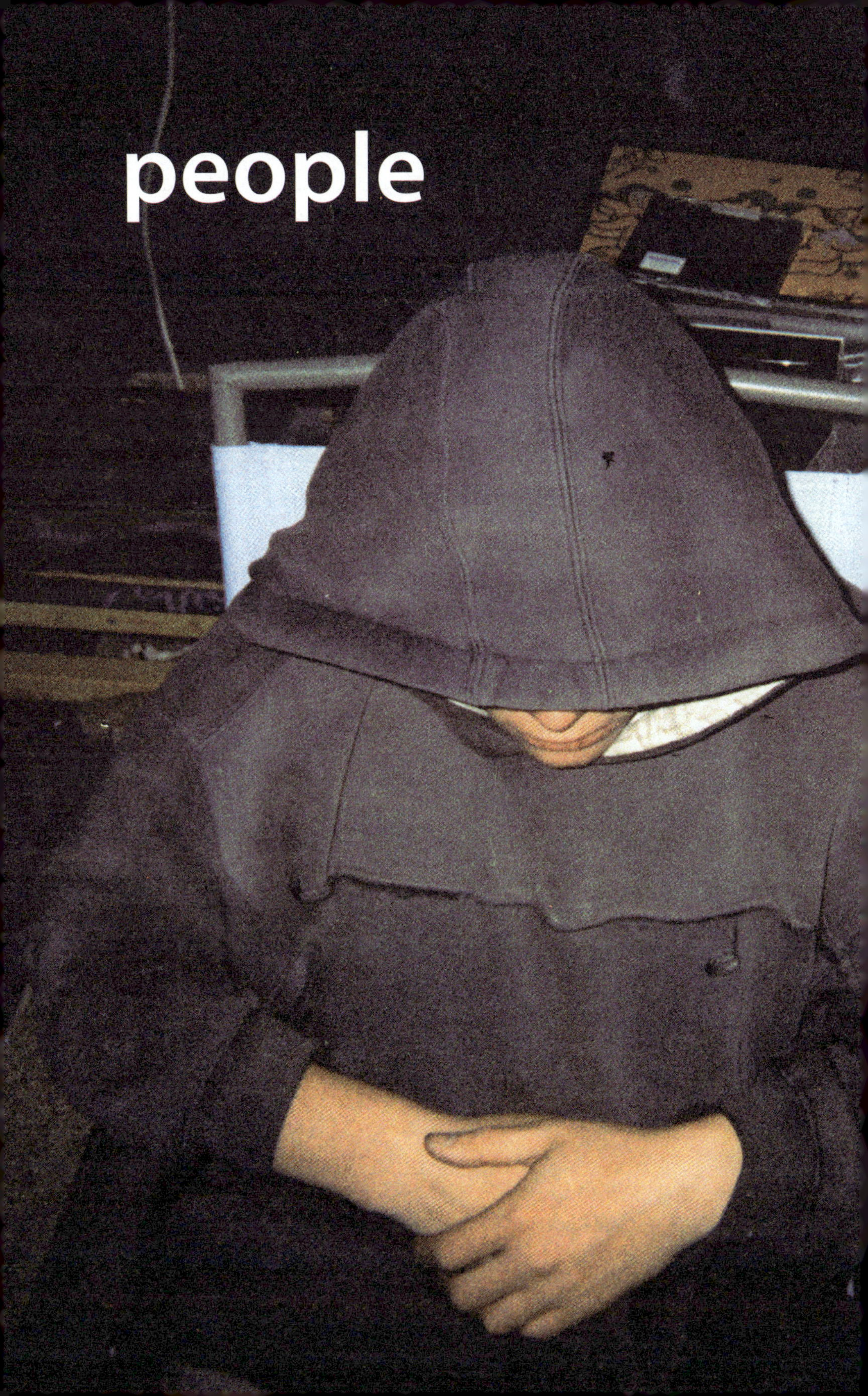
people

When I think about being hopeful I think about being with my girlfriend and my Mum. They bring tranquility and calmness. They make me calmer, which makes me hopeful. I don't do the calm thing very well. I'm usually very aggro. Hopefully in the future I can see myself being different. I'll have a job and I'll have my anger under control. Sometimes I go off the deep end a bit. People staring at me makes me angry. I'd just like people's respect.

The police make me angry. The very presence of them makes me furious. I hate them. They lock my Mum up all the time. So I've hated them all my life. If I could imagine being with anyone it would be my Mum. She makes me feel safe. She knows what to say. She's always been there, unless she's in gaol. I think what my Mum would want for my future is for me to read and write and make a good wage and see me happy.

The people who're important to me help me by keeping me calm and keeping me out of gaol. I've been in gaol. It's probably a black mark on my future. But it pointed me in the right direction, I think, because I didn't want to be there. I want to give myself a good future. I want to have money in my pocket. I don't want to have to go out and steal money and steal things. I want to be a bricklayer. A builder. I like the work. My Mum can help me with that.

No-one really gave a shit about me in the past. They think I'm just a druggie who's going down and I've got a bit of a bad mouth. My anger could get in the way of my future. And the police. Everyone else has knocked me down already so I'm glad to get back up from it. When my mum was in gaol I ended living at friends' places and they just steal from you and ended up kicking me out and keeping everything that I owned. So I just lived here, there and everywhere. All I hope for is that I have a job. I don't know if it will come true.

Some people just think that we should know better, so to speak. But we haven't been taught another way. So we don't know another way. We haven't had another way. So for the future that means we'll end up being drug dealers. I don't want to be a drug dealer. Been there done that.

If I work for the money I'm not going to go and spend it all on pot, I might like to go and buy some gold, or clothes, something nice, something I can keep, hold on to.

I've done the other future. My mother was a drug dealer her whole life. And then she went to gaol. That put it into perspective for me. We used to be sitting pretty. We had everything we wanted. But now we've got nothing, we're living in a car. I don't want that. I want to have money. I don't want the cops to be able to take it from me. I want to say 'no, it's not drug money mate, look, I fuckin' worked mate, this is my fuckin' house, get fucked'. I want to show everyone—the people who kicked me out when my Mum was in gaol—stick it to them all, fuck them. I don't need them, I can do it on my own.

Hopefully I'll have a decent future. Hopefully I've got a connection with a decent builder. And a job. In 20 years hopefully I'm a builder with a child. He won't have fuckin' drug addict for a mother and he won't have a drug addict for a father. And he'll always have that option, that he has the freedom to do what he likes, and he also has the comfort of his family around. I'd like my Mum to be standing with me.

In the future I want a house. That's all I want. A house that's mine and no-one can take it away from me. I want my child and my family to know that I'm not a stuff-up. I want to have an everyday life like you see in a fuckin' movie.

HOPE IS THE NEW BEGINNING, what's coming to the future, what we're going to see, what our pathway is going to be.

I felt hopeful about being born.

Last year was the worst year of my life. I lost my best friend with a mistake, and then two weeks ago, she called me up and now we're talking again, as she's realised it was the guy, and it wasn't me. And she put me through so much hell. I couldn't go to the Plaza or anything because she wanted to smash me.

I like school. That's where my friends are. My mum's hugs make me feel hopeful, like a little princess.

I'm going to get a hairdressing job, I can see it already. I'm going to start off my life.

The closest things to me are probably my family and my friends. If I didn't have them in my life, I would probably be crashing down at the moment. I'm on depression pills. If I didn't have the support of my family I think I would have gone through a breakdown.

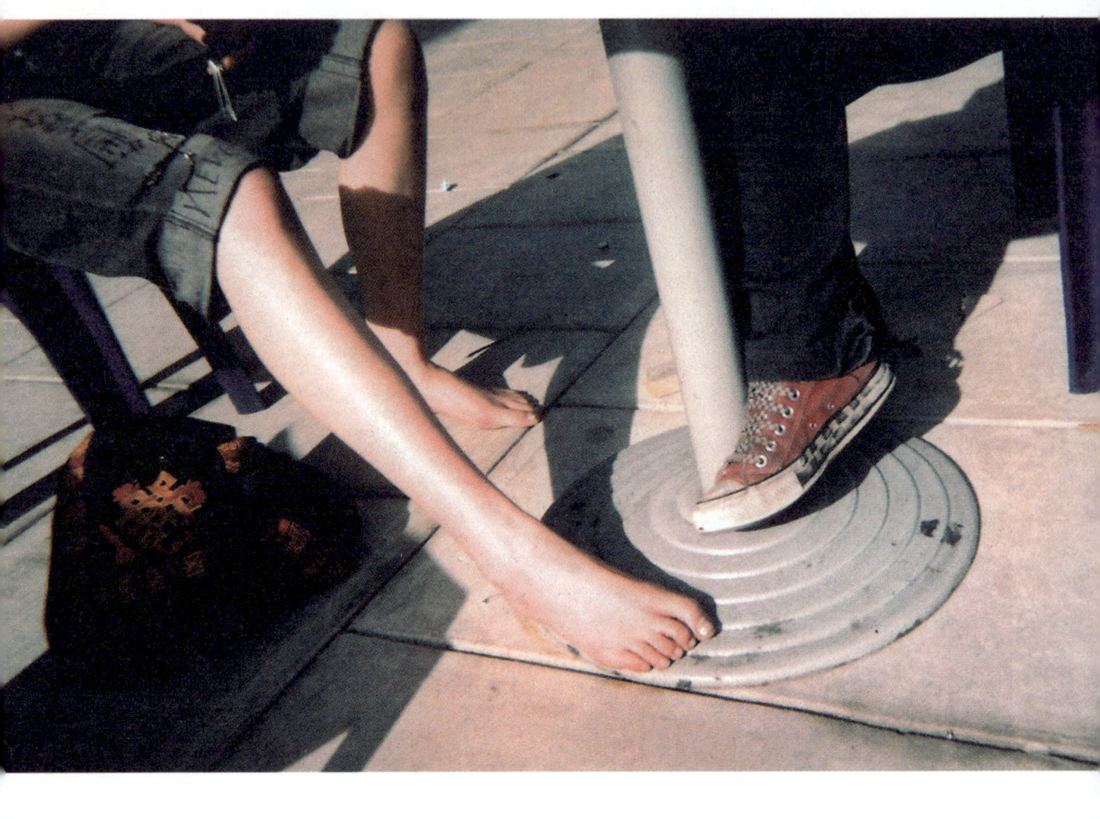

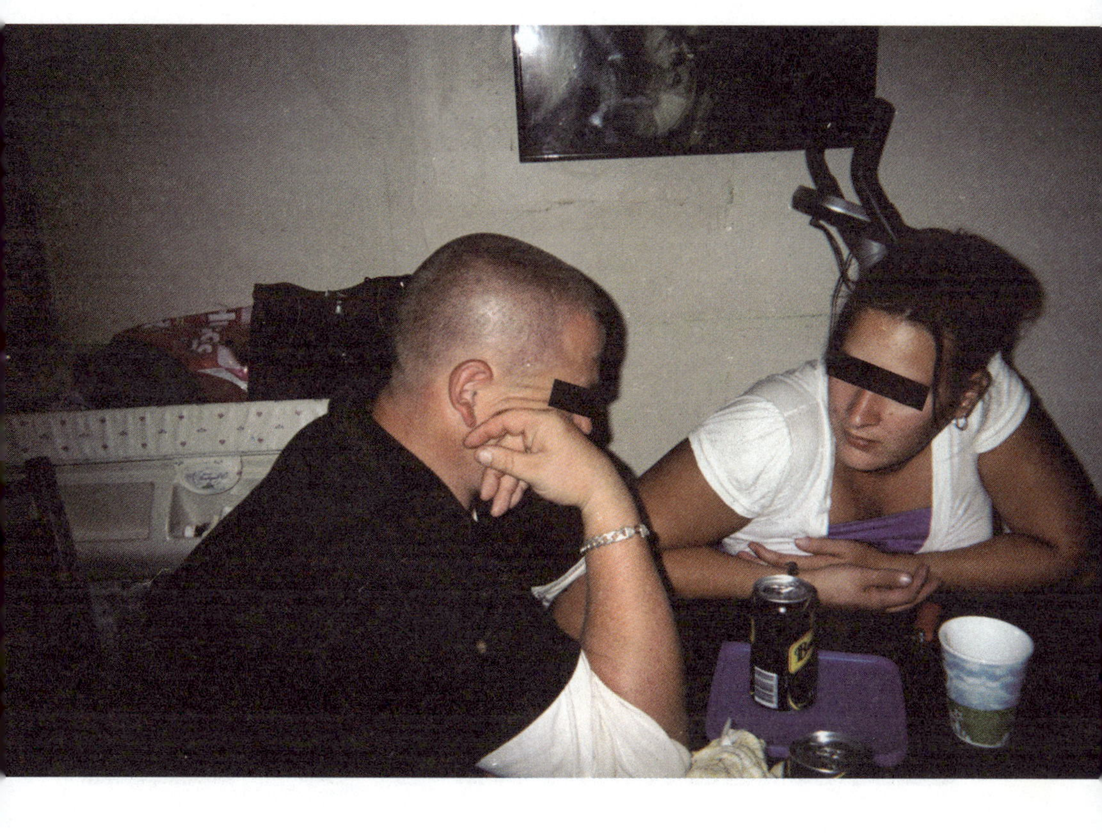

When I remember moments of feeling hopeful I think about the time I formed my relationship again with my mum. Me and my mum just we didn't get along. We had a big fight, and we weren't speaking, and I didn't want nothing to do with her, and then she got put into hospital, and then I started talking to her again, and that's when I felt hopeful, like I might be able to have a relationship with her.

School is a hopeful place for me because that's where I've got my true friends. I found out what true friends are, they're not back stabbers, they're actually there for you, they're not there for what you have or what's around you, or what environment you're living in, they're actually there for you.

I feel hopeful when I'm with my dad.

TOP SPIN

I WANT TO BE A RECEPTIONIST because I don't need an apprenticeship.

With my future, I have to make a choice, whether it's going to be good or bad, and I haven't yet made that choice, so once I've made that choice, that's when I'll know if I'm going to be good, or turn out bad.

The only reason I'd chose a bad future would be because of my boyfriend. If I'm gonna stay with my boyfriend then I can already see it's going to turn out to be a bad future, because I can see he's going to go nowhere. He's 18 and he's got no life, he does nothing except sit at home all day. He doesn't think of the future. He doesn't want a good future. He doesn't talk about having a good future, all he talks about is having a bad future, and violence, and anger, and scary things.

He's important to me, deep down, but I need to move on. I'm going to have to let go of love, and make the toughest choice I can make, and just be there for myself, nobody else. I've got to be there for myself before I can help anybody else.

My boyfriend's mum taught me you can't have no respect for nobody else if you don't have respect for yourself first. You can't help anybody else, or you can't help yourself if you don't want to help yourself first.

That's about developing a sense of hopefulness for yourself.

What's important to me is my parents and my family. My Mum's important to me. Anyone that helps me. Sometimes I hit the bottom and sometimes it takes a long time to come back up. If I start going downhill then I really go downhill. Drugs probably make me go down. And shit not going my way. And sometimes a row of things that just doesn't go your way.

In the future I want to see myself doing something good. Not something pointless. I don't really want to be one of those people that doesn't really like what they're doing. I think you have to enjoy what you're doing. The good thing I'm hoping for is a steady job. I like cars. Doing up cars or something like that.

People who I want to be part of my future are loyal. Most of my friends are pretty loyal people. I don't like dishonest people. Not controlling myself right gets in the way of my future. It just leads to bad stuff. Cops can get involved. Most people can get along without having trouble with dickheads.

It's good to take memories of learning forward into the future. In the future I wouldn't mind being a dad. But I'd want to be better than my Dad. I could give advice. I can see myself with a hot missus.

I don't reckon the world is going to be around much longer. I can see the changes in the weather. Heaps of new wars will come. My generation's not going take it much more. Not much in Iraq has changed. Or in Afghanistan. I don't think they show you half the stuff that goes on. It makes the future hard to see. I like having somewhere to go where I don't have to think about anything. Somewhere I can just be myself and not worry about anything. I like to go to this huge building where you can walk around, from sun up to sun down, just walking around with torches and looking. It's heaps quite and you can clear your mind.

There's some mad pieces around. If you get bored you can just look at the art. They've taken heaps of fun stuff away from kids. There's no way you can get a rush in life without breaking the law. Speeding in a car gives me the biggest rush. Seeing shit flying past you and you're holding onto the wheel like you're making it do it. I need to have a rush. Graphing is pretty good. You have to be sneaky and there's always an element of getting caught. I don't do it on anyone's home though. That wouldn't be right.

DTD

places

At the moment I try and keep myself together with this hope of going to university, and completing a degree and stuff, but I don't see that happening now. The fact is that we might not be able to afford it, for me to go. There's only me and Mum, so we can't really afford for me to go to uni. I'd probably do a science degree of some sort.

I've been told I'm lucky to get a dead-end job at a supermarket being a checkout girl.

I've got cats at home, and I like to feed them and cuddle them and stuff, and pat them. I suppose that gets me through sometimes when I'm upset. And then there's a fish that needs to be fed.

Going to university will get me a great job. I'd earn enough money that I could maybe adopt one of those children that you see on those World Vision ads.

Some people see me as a green Martian because of my disorders, like my ADD and my ODD—Oppositional Defiance Disorder. No one can touch me. I'm poisonous or something. It makes me angry.

People think that uni's not going to happen at all, and I'm very angry at that as well.

I like going to the Japanese Garden in the parklands. It's pretty. I'd take some of my homework and I'd go and sit by the sea of pebbles, there in that little shelter, because it was so quiet, and then I'd just work, quietly. When there's a down time, I just sit there and I think 'One day I could be at university. One day I could be doing this. One day I could be in Italy watching a soccer match', like I've always wanted. You don't know what's going to just be given to you, or what life is going to bring. So you've just got to keep yourself there.

ONE
WAY

I PLAN TO BE A PARK RANGER. I've got about five years of uni after school. And when I get a job in park ranging hopefully I'll probably try to start up in comedy. Once I've saved up enough money I plan to move over to Canada. What's hopeful about my future in Canada is park ranging and comedy. I just bought a video camera on eBay. Me and my friend are planning to do a comedy thing on community TV.

Canada is such a big place full of parks. That's why I want to go there. I wouldn't say it's hopeful. How can you say what makes you hopeful? It's not one particular thing. Hope to me is, like, I hope I get past the next level in a computer game.

What's important to me at the moment is my life. After that it would be my best friend.

I'd like to bring comedy to the world.

I live in a motel where a carer is paid to look after me. A different carer comes on every eight hours.

My Mum's with me all the way. I'm not one of those people that needs lots of friends. If I was to become rich and famous I'd still keep in contact with my friends. I don't need other people telling me what hope is. What's got me through all my struggles is me.

On my birthday my mother was supposed to give me $100, but instead she spent it on alcohol and the pokies. But I didn't ask her about it because she'd just lost her best friend. I didn't accept what she did, but I understood why she did it.

I used to get really angry. Whenever I get angry now I turn it into humour instead.

In the future I want to travel. I don't really need hope because I just know it's going to happen. I'm saving my money, working one step at a time, getting closer to doing what I want to do. There's a few of my friends I'd like to be with in the future. The people I don't want to be part of my future I've already kicked them out of my life. Lots and lots of people in my family, lots of my old friends, people I used to hang around with, they're just annoying because they piss me off. I tell them to piss off. I don't have time for people to waste my time and shit. I don't like taking shit from anybody, it just annoys me.

There's been some tough times but you get over it and move on, deal with the cards you get dealt. I've got myself on drugs before, I do it very occasionally. I just get myself into a rut, and I just can't see anything in the future, and it gets really bad and I can't see myself getting out of that rut, and I can't get work, I just get frustrated by being in Adelaide, and I just get frustrated and I can't think of anything else, but generally I don't really know how I get out of them, I just sort of sort it out myself, deal with it, and move on.

Some people start to define the future and plan for it. Other people just go through school, and most people, like people I hang around with just say 'Yeah, whatever happens, happens, just deal with it as it comes'. I don't really know if I see myself that far in the future. I just want to travel, that's about it.

I'm paranoid about everyone; I don't trust anyone. I trust my friends to a certain degree but I still don't trust them as much as I probably should. The stuff that's important to me I usually keep on me at all times. In the future I want to look back and say 'Well I did what the hell I wanted to do right then', I'll be perfectly happy with that because I was happy my whole life, rather than spending, like, five years of uni, hating it, just so I could be happy in five years. With my friends it doesn't matter where we go or what we do as long as we have fun along the way.

But where you end up is the problem. In 20 years time I'd like to be dead. But that might change in the future. All the adults keep saying 'You're not going to think that when you're older' and shit like that. That really pisses me off. I'm just saying that to adults to shut them up, they piss me off, because I say I don't really want to live to old age, I really don't.

I don't really know what old age will be, but I can imagine myself getting really bored with life and killing myself, not like in a depressed way, but in a way that's 'I'm bored with life'.

I don't really know because I don't know what's going to happen in my life. The future and your actions that happen in future and the past don't matter, it's what's in the present that matters.

What pisses me off is other people bringing drama into my life. People dying, that pisses me off, especially when I don't know them and I don't care. I don't care about people that are mourning. Relationships annoy the hell out of me. I hate relationships. I haven't had a relationship in ages just because I've seen people around me and they get so worked up over a good relationship, it's frustrating. I'll have time for that shit when I'm older. I really don't have time for drama. If people think I'm going to change for any reason, they can get fucked. In the future I'll stand up for what I believe in and I'm not going to change just from some dickhead that comes along.

There's a garden with large trees, grass, dappled light and flowers. The garden smells clean. The garden is reached by traveling a long hard walk where the walker moves away from civilization. It's a secret garden, it's a silent place, without people, a garden located in the future.

There's a giant hillside or cliff. On the edge of the cliff is a large tree, an elm or oak. This place is called 'A tribute to humans'.

There's a place where there's a car park in a shopping mall. It's day time. There's two cars parked next to a McDonald's. The cars are new. There's no one around except for a man walking somewhere in the background. This place is called 'The new cars'.

There's a place where all the prime ministers in the world bring their flags and burn them. Then they all hold up a flag with a peace sign inside an orange triangle.

There's a lounge room. In the lounge room is my mother, my aunty, my little sisters and brothers, and a baby. Mum and aunty are having coffee. The kids are playing X Box 'Resident evil'. The adults are talking about me, about how to help me. They're kind. In the room there are poems: 'I want you to love me' and 'Love Me'. There's splashing coming from the pool outside. This place is called 'Feelings that flow along'.

A girl is driving with her friends to a nice party, where there are lots of nice people, friendly people that all have lives and have jobs and that will go to work every week day, and then come home on the weekend and think, 'we can let ourselves go now'.

In a place that's 'hot' there's models draped over cars, there are cigarettes all over the floor, there's money on the floor and money hanging from the ceiling. There's fluffy dice inside the car and the models are primo models in fishnet stockings.

There's a room where an enormous glass cube is suspended from the ceiling. There are breathing holes in the top of the cube. Inside the cube are more cubes. Inside these cubes are drug addicts separated by glass from drugs. This is happening in the future where there is no food.

future

When I think about hope I think about dope plants. And money. I can see myself in a hydro. I'm watering the plants. I've got ten grand in my pocket everywhere I go. I've got a crop out the backyard. My mates are there. I'm living in a two-story house in Two Wells. On two acres. My mates are working for me watering my plants. I need a big pair of lights, some water that trickles, fans. I need some money to buy the equipment. Right now I grow vegetables in my backyard. I grow tomatoes and rockmelon.

The people who are important to me are my dad, my brothers, my Nan and Pop. A special place for me is the carport at home. We've got a pool table and shit.

Asians are getting in the way of my future. They keep slicing up my mates with big machetes, all over the place, in my area, in my house and shit. They're overtaking my area. You've got to run from them or else they'll chop you. They're all schizophrenic because they think we're talking about them.

In the future there wouldn't be any Asians. They'd all be shot by skinheads.

AF
FUCK OFF

What's important to me about the future is my art work. One day I hope to have a clothes brand of my own. So I can compete with the popular brands. Have a real big name. I know I've got the right styles for it. Everyone wants the T-shirts I make. It's always been a goal to get my own brand. Ever since I started drawing I've wanted it. There's no-one really who's going to help me get there. I'll do it myself.

There's not really anyone in my life at the moment that I want next to me in the future. My parents haven't been supportive enough over the last couple of years. I just see myself doing it on my own. It pisses me off that my parents don't support me as much as they used to, they're good parents, but they just don't give a shit when they see something that I do. I don't pay much attention to it. I just ignore it.

I hate thinking about the future at this stage of my life. It's frustrating. I can't see myself in the future. I'm going to have to try hard and think about it and don't do nothing stupid. Try to keep control. Keep calm for the future.

2005

FUTUTE
Bomings

My Mum keeps me hopeful because she loves me. My sisters are still hopeful because they try and get me doing things, and try get me to school, and tell me I should, tell me I should do it or else I'm not going to have a future, I'm going to be a bum, but I don't really see myself having a future.

In the future I think we'll all be dead because the sun could have burnt us. So we're going to die. I don't know, I really don't know about the future.

If I could have a future I'd have a big house. It would be big and have flowers and trees. And a car. And I'd want my Mum to be there. Mainly my Mum, my family, would be there. My friends. My pets. My bed. My room. My computer.

I like it on the net and I like talking to my friends on MSN.

Stoned for the future

What's important to me is my family, that's it. My nephews and my niece. They're my babies. Friends are important too but not as much as family. The word 'hope' means nothing to me. The future's hard to imagine because there could be lots of different things. Most people think that I'm not going to do anything with my life. I don't know what I'm going to do. In the future there might be everyone in my family, just my family. Maybe a partner, kids, who knows?

I don't really have a hopeful place, because my house burnt down a few months ago, and that was the only place that I felt comfortable and everything. I keep wishing that I could go back, I could just go home. I lived there for five years, so everything sort of happened there. Mostly bad things happened there, but I was living there when my nephew was born. My bedroom was big, it was nice. I had a poster of Emenem on the wall.

I love the movie Titanic. I love that movie, I cry every time. It takes me a lot to cry. I cry in the part where she lets him go, and he just like goes under the water, and then—well that part sort makes you upset, but then at the end you see all the people when they're alive again, when they're alive and stuff.

I don't watch TV. I don't surf on the Internet, I just talk on MSN. It makes me feel normal, that's all.

People can, like, comfort you and shit, but in the end you're by yourself, you have to do everything by yourself.

In the future I want to be rich. In the future I want to be successful, and just to be happy and healthy. That matters more than being wealthy, and have a nice house, and have a good job. Staying at school, that really helps, just doing my job, the job I have at the moment, which is coming to school every morning, on time, and staying in my lessons. That counts, that will affect my future.

I like interacting with people, so I think I want to do something where you see people every day, like a receptionist, because they have people come in every day, they get to meet new people. Life always has its ups and downs, and there are times where you probably feel more hopeful than others.

What helps me is, I think, that there's always something around the corner, I always think that there's always something around the corner, and that's something that keeps me going. I guess that is being hopeful too.

In ten years time I'll be 23 years old, so I should have a job by then, and have a phone, not my own house, but a tempo house until I get a really good one. That's what I hope. Family and friends are very important in your life. And if you don't have anyone to talk to you'll have a lot of mental breakdowns.

A lot of young people look up to their parents, and like, you know, you say 'Oh, when I get older I want to, I want to have one of these like my Mum, and I want to like live there, like my Mum'. Like a lot of young people, like, look up to their parents, so they'd hope in the future to be like them, kind of.

I don't have the time to think about stuff like an ideal house or an ideal bedroom. My life is busy. I live in a motel, so I don't really get to decide what bedroom I have, but it's not important to me, as long as I have a place to sleep. I have another house, which is my bedroom, which is nice, but bedrooms I don't think are very important to me. I like to socialise with my friends, go shopping. There's no particular place that's important to me.

A lot of parents want you to be what they failed to be. My friend's mother, she really wanted to be like be a ballet dancer, but she broke her toe, and she couldn't do it, so when her daughter was born she's like, 'You have to be a ballet dancer'. And she was pushing her daughter to do it and her daughter didn't want to be a ballet dancer, and the child had to say, 'Mum, that's what you want, that's not what I want'. And parents don't like that. They don't think about what the children want. What children want in the future is money and cigarettes and cars and hot models draped over cars smoking cigarettes. I want all my friends to be in my future, and my family.

But I don't see the future. Children aren't psychics.

When i think about the future I think about what sort of house I'm going to live in, what sort of animals I'm going to have, and what friends I'm going to have. I want to become a vet or work with animals. That's my target for life.

In ten years time I can see myself having a house of my own, not having any kids, having a husband perhaps, and having a big yard for the sick animals that need help, and then when they get better, letting them go.

My one priority that I want in life is to be able to help all the animals out there, and to become someone who drives around in a car and picks up wild animals and brings them back so they can get fixed up. And then you release them.

I've already got my own farm at home. I've been helping the sick animals out there already, like the magpies, the dogs, rabbits, cats. I bring them home and my puppy, who is my baby, I raised him, he's got a sore on his shoulder at the moment, so I've been fixing that and it's going away. I just have a thing for animals. I can get along with animals more than I can humans.

The animals come to me for their help, so I give them my help, and then I release them. If they need to be put down, I get them put down. If I see them getting sick I get them put down, because I can't do it myself.

My Mum is getting sick of me talking about the animals, and I don't talk about animals to new people that I've just met because they think I'm sort of a baby. I was called a little kid because I was walking home from school with my friends, or people, and a little bird fell in front of my feet out of a nest, and I took it home and fed it, and then released it, and then a rumour started around the school saying I'm a little girl still, at the age of 13. I'm not a little girl. And I was getting into fights. Those people were getting in the way of my future.

Right from the age when I was little, I've been able to have a thing for animals. If I see sickness in an animal I cry.

My future is to help the animals out there, and I've already looked into my future, saving up all my pocket money, putting it into the bank account.

I'm having fences up around a whole big property, and having cages for dogs to go into when they're sick, having stuff for cows and horses, when they've got sore legs. I'd be able to help them, and I'd release them in the wild again. That's what I want. Only one thing, I don't know where I'm going to get all the money from.

I've already achieved what I wanted in life, so I just keep going on about the future. I'm not going to worry about kids, I'm going to worry about the sick animals out there. When I was younger I wanted kids. Now I've got older I don't want them because I want to have the animals. They're going to be my kids.

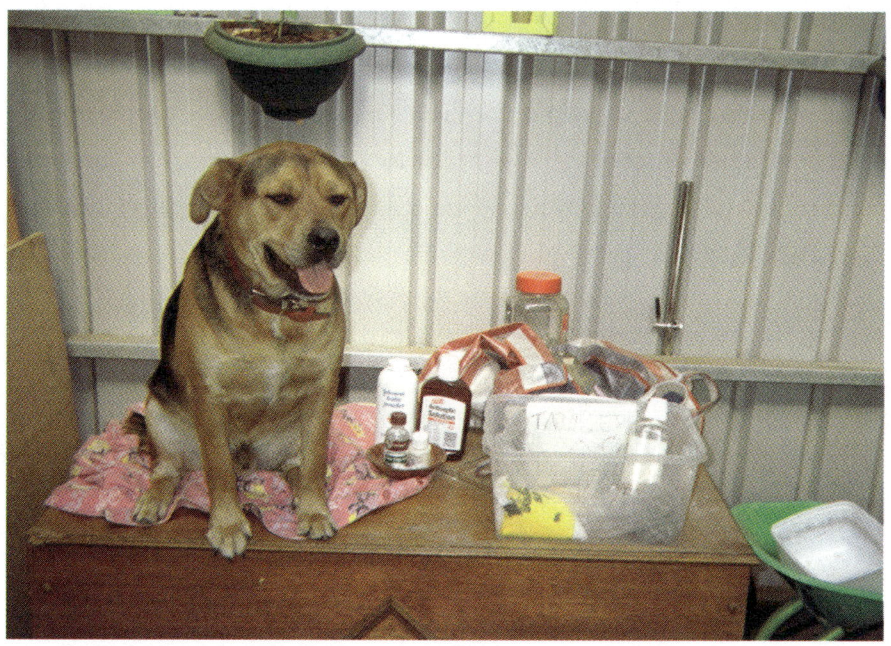

You need support from your family otherwise you're going to find it hard. You've got to have support all the way.

Everyone's got a different point of view on shit. The fuckin' cops have a negative view about my future. You get in trouble once you get in shit more. Your family wants what's best for you and the cops don't really give a fuck. My Mum and my mates and some cops know how tough things have been for me. Some cops would know because when shit used to happen they'd come round and help me out.

In 20 years I can see myself with a nice job, a fuckin' pimped-out fuckin' car, a hot little bitch, maybe kids. I want a house. I'd bring my kids up better than I was. I was brought up alright but I fucked around heaps. Instead of having a flash car I'd rather have kids with a good upbringing. I'd like my kids to go to school where they can set up their future from a young age. Your future, and whether you've got a job and shit, depends on what you do now. That's where I really fucked my life up, but I feel like I can rescue that now.

In the future I'll either get a job and be working, or be in Yatala, or dead.

With most of us, like, where I come from, all of us are Aboriginals, we all stick together, like to us we're all family, if a fun thing happens, we all go for it, and most of us, we either go to school, do our share, and then we go to get a job, if not we either do drugs, steal, and then like the next, the next step from that is in Magill, and that's where most of my cousins are, and I've been there, most of my other cousins have, and there's only one cousin I actually know so far who's actually, like, going to school and doing the right thing, and that's, like, my little brother. All the rest of us have all been through the hard roads and stuff, and with us, with our family, you can't get nothing for free.

If you want something you always have to do it yourself, and that's how we all like were raised. We were brought up on the streets, we learnt how to do what we need to do to survive.

That's what we usually do, but then you just get all fucked up from television, watching all this like global warming shit, all this war going on and everything, and then that's what like really starts to fuck with your head, and with most of us we like look at it, and then hear of all this shit saying 'Well yeah, we're going to like, they're all going to be big floods, we can all die from hurricanes and shit', and after that kicks in you just start snapping, start going, like you snap at anybody. So is it, like, every man for themselves. You might as well just give up and do whatever.

With me and my cousin last year, when we first heard about the global warming stuff come in, that's when I first snapped and I was like starting to schiz out, and then when that happened I used to be up in town every night, like driving around in somebody's car and bashing, like bashing guys on the streets, and then after that, I just stopped, because the weed really pushed me onto the edge, and from there I was either going to be back in Magill or dead, from the way I was going, and then after I just snapped out of it, went all straight, and then my cousin did as well.

If I could have any sort of future that I wanted, I'd probably be living in a home, just living in a big house, just working doing weapons design, maybe biological weapons. They've got them out in Woomera: bio-weaponry services.

I love watching the old movies, like Hostel, watching people get cut up. I don't know why, I just like watching it. That's when I start thinking of designing guns, or designing knives or something. I like watching people getting cut up and stuff so I think, well, it would be a good idea to get like paid to do that kind of stuff.

Nobody knows what I want for my future because most of the time I always keep to myself, but there's only a few people I really like and let out to, and that's my mum, my brothers and sisters, and my first cousin.

Others just see my future the way it has been. We were always doing the same old stuff, running around, running amok on the streets and stuff, and with them I'm always usually the quiet one at the back, but if anything happened I'd be the first one in and the last one out. I would be the one who, like, starts it, and I'll be the one who finishes it. I don't see any of them in my future. All my cousins I reckon now they're going to jail or they're going to be dead.

The most important people to me in my life at the moment are my mum and my brother and sisters, and my first cousin. I can see them being with me in the future I want. My mum supports me with anything, but with my brothers and sisters, they'll listen to you but they won't get too involved with you.

With crime, with shit like that, you can't back down from nothing with all my boys. If you do that then, like, they just look at you like you're a bitch and they'll just like smack you around or something, tell you to fuck off. That's how it is.

Like when you're with them, you either do it, you have to be, like, quick, one mind, in and out, and that's it. At first it was like I was excited and stuff, and then after a while it started getting scary, and then started getting used to it, and then it started getting boring, and then when I got locked up I just went all for hell, I just thought 'Oh to hell with it', and when I got out stopped it for a little bit, and then got back into it, and then the cops came around and they said that 'Oh yeah, we know like they did it' and everything 'And we're just going to get your DNA and we're going to get you', try and like play mind games with me, and I was like 'Yeah, whatever', and then they went off, and then after that I just stopped it. I haven't touched nothing.

With all my aunties and everything, when they talk about my future, they always reckon like, you've got the goods, you could go out there and do it. But then there's the people, the people that I hang around with, and I know that some of them are like me who always gets dragged into it, where all we want to do is just sit at home with each other, watch movies or something, or go out, nothing like go out stealing and shit, like, just go out to movies and something, and then as soon as all the other boys come around it's like 'Yeah, come on, let's go steal a car', so we tried like stop them, like, we tried not to, but they always end up doing it, we always end up tagging along.

The place that makes me feel hopeful is my neighbourhood. That's the only place. I mean where my house is and everything, because everybody lives near, like all my uncles and aunties and everything, they all live near me, so that means it's only a street away to go see one of my cousins, or the house down the road, just to go and see my mum's sister or something, because we're all real close together and we're all in the same neighbourhood, we're all out, all the time, always with each other, and it's just real safe, so it doesn't matter if something's happened over at my house, I could just stay at one of my cousin's house to sleep, and if they're not there, then somewhere else, and it's always real good.

My mum reckons I'm like my dad. I don't like hanging out with women. They're too much trouble.

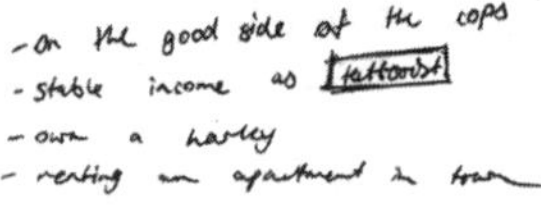

In the future I'll probably get an apprenticeship or something. If there's anyone that might get in the way of this it might be me. I've got to go to school and I can't drop out. The police get in the way, when you get in trouble and shit. They just prevent you from doing shit that you want to do. In 20 years time I can see myself with my own house, sitting on the couch and watching TV. Maybe kids. I want a car too. I'd want my kids to be good people. I'd want my kids to be strong and shit so they can stick up for themselves like I've had to stick up for myself.

teachers

I did many years of mainstream teaching and found myself being drawn to the kids who were at the fringes. There were plenty of teachers taking care of the big core. I was interested in the people who were dislocated, the graffiti offenders, the odd ones out, the geeks, and I focused on those instinctively.

When I work with the kids I'm completely aware that they have a long history of being dishonest, that they are capable of displaying extreme behaviours, and sometimes behaviours that I don't even see coming. I work being very mindful of that reality, and then I begin a slow process of chipping that away and getting rid of that rough exterior, of finding the other things that are more important, the core of those people, those individuals, then bringing that forth, helping those things to blossom, and it's a very patient process.

Maintaining relationships with the kids is just like you do with any friend, you treat the kids like friends. You take an interest in your friends, you enquire after them, and you remember their birthdays, you remember the names of their siblings, and their mothers and fathers, and if you don't see them for a while and you catch up 'Oh, how's your mother going?' knowing that X's mother had been locked up for drug offences, and has been released, or saying 'Do you need any food? We put a food parcel together for you to take home. How are you going?' It's a genuine concern, saying it and then telling them 'It's OK, you're at rock bottom here but we'll sort this out, I've got these things in place, we can do these things. You shower, you get clean, here's some clean clothes'. We'll find them some money to get some food and some clothes for them. It's about just being a genuine friend to them.

What I'd like to see in the future for these kids varies. For some it's survival. Maybe eventually some sense of normalcy, whatever that is. It might just be some part-time work, some income, and a nice safe place to live, and the ability to have strong, healthy relationships with the opposite sex, and friends and family, a sense of being normal.

I suspect that numbers of my kids have graduated to the adult prison system, which is very frightening for them, but that's sadly what happens. I'm not about trying to save them, because I can't, they have to save themselves. Some will end up having a pretty despairing existence, and that will revolve around drug abuse and drug addiction. No matter what we do that won't change

To create a sense of hope in the future for them is probably the hardest thing of all.

Hopefulness means an incredible amount to me. When I look at my life and the things that I've experienced I now have incredible hope for myself and for the young people here. I've suffered with mental illness and drug addiction. I've been institutionalised for these things in my life, and the latest one was three years ago, so I feel really proud of what I am today, and I have incredible hope for my future, for my life.

I had always been intent on doing harm to myself and not wanting to live, but I reached a point where I thought I want to be happy and enjoy my life. My family, who are incredibly supportive, and a few close friends that I have thought that I would never even make it to the age I am. And they look at me now and just say 'Wow!' you have come so far, and I have, I really have. I guess I always knew that they believed in me, and that's important I think, if there's someone that can say to you 'You're OK, and I believe in you, I have faith, I'm here for you'. A lot of these kids don't have that. A really big thing that gets in the way of the future for these kids is that not many of them have parental support. They don't have a mum or a dad that will say, 'It's important that you get to school today', because often they don't care.

For these kids the future is something that doesn't belong to them. It's coming from somewhere else, from an institution like school. Or the future is having fun with their friends and smoking pot, and getting drunk on the weekend. They say 'It doesn't matter because I won't be alive anyway'. There's a lot of death, a lot of drugs.

There's a lot of pressure to achieve outcomes, to get these kids job-ready and get them out there. But they're not job-ready at all, and pushing them isn't going to help. Push them and they'll work at Coles for a week before they tell the boss to shove it, and they'll be angry, and they'll steal, so you can't push them.

I think a lot of them are depressed and probably don't know it, and don't recognise it. They don't have any sense of self-worth. I don't think they can look at themselves and say 'I deserve to have a good life, and a long life, a happy life, and to get a job'. They don't think they're worthy of that, and I don't think you can tell them 'Well you are', they need to work that out, and hopefully they will. I have hope and faith that they will work it out one day.

I WAS TALKING TO ANOTHER STAFF MEMBER THE OTHER NIGHT, about our position here, as mentors, as teachers, as educators, and we were talking about how some young people come back. For me that's the highlight because it's like planting seeds, when the young people come back and share those success stories with us. And then there was a knock on the door, and a young person who hadn't been at the school for about five years opens the door and says 'Hello! Do you remember me?' And of course we remembered the child, and asked what he was doing. He was working as a rigger, and he was doing rigging lights for various pop concerts, sporting events, and was travelling Australia doing all this rigging. He was totally over the moon about the job he was doing. He said if it wasn't for us, steering him back on the right path, he probably wouldn't have got his act together, and wouldn't have thought about his future and what he might be doing.

I have seen the success stories, and that spurs you on, and even when things are going rough, at the back of your mind you know that if you keep supporting them, you keep showing them the right path, if you keep being a mentor, and walk for a moment in their shoes as well, rather than coming from middle class values, that holds you in good stead to continue to motivate you, long term.

I had cross-roads in my life as well, where I could have gone one way or another, and if it wasn't for a couple of key people, one being a physical education teacher (and I became a physical education teacher) so those key people plant those seeds, and I hold those names and those people dear to my heart, and that spurs me on.

POKIES

My first three months here was the hardest time I ever experienced as a teacher, because I had to get rid of all my other thoughts. You had a persona that you've had for 20-odd years, and you've got to drop it because it doesn't work here, and it's very confronting. I found it one of the most confronting things I've done in my life, one of the hardest journeys, it was a really tough journey for me, personally, because it was so alien to anything that I'd done before. I thought it was going to be really hard for me, and it is, and it's still a battle because of my type of personality.

The only way it works here is the power of your relationships. That's what I've found. And that's a good thing, that's a nice thing, it's a nice feeling to have. They sit in the front seat next to you, they talk to you while you're driving, and I do a lot of that because I'm taking them out of the school, and that's a nice feeling, it's companionable, and it's free-flowing, and it's just like you're with your friends or anyone else, so there's no barrier at all. But I had a situation this week that affected me in a negative way, because of the relations I've built up with one kid here. There was a situation during the week where another student was abusive to a teacher in a really full-on way, and I said 'It's alright, don't let it get to you, just take a walk', you know, 'cool down'. 'No, no, no', he's going on and on, and I said 'we'll sort it out'. This kid that I had the good relationship with was wandering around. I mean I spent a bit of time trying to settle this other one down, and he just comes in and he says 'Yeah, why don't you go and smack her in the head', and he was talking about the new female teacher here, and that was a real trigger for me. I got really angry, and this is with a kid that I've got a really great relationship with. I got furious, straight off. I said 'That's not on. I'm not accepting that. I'm sending you home', and I was really angry and I was going to start a lesson and he ended up following me out and then started to say a few things, and then he gives me a hard time for the whole lesson when we were out there playing volleyball and I say 'You're making this worse. I'm asking you to go to your lesson', and I was really still trying to calm myself down, and then he got personally abusive to me like 'Suck my dick'. This is this kid I had this great relationship with. I got confused, conflicting relations. I'm really angry with what he said. He's inciting this other kid to violence, and this other kid is very, very violent, and we've had a lot of problems with him. That kid did not get sent home, which is what we try and do when behaviour is unacceptable, because when we've tried to do that in the past it up-ends everything in the school, smashing things, creating a huge drama, so rather than have that happen again, he actually stayed and then we suspended him, and I didn't agree with that because in a way I feel as if they get away with that behaviour if they don't have that immediate consequence, 'We're not tolerating staff abuse, or threats to the staff', but we didn't follow that through because we were concerned of his reaction to it, because he's done it in the past...

I was disappointed that the kid I had a good relationship with started abusing me, and I didn't feel that until that night even, but I knew that I was angry and I was upset, but I didn't really understand why, but I knew it was to do with feeling he's let me down.

No matter how good that relationship is, that if it's put on the line, if their friends are involved, they'll wipe you. You might think that you've got a good relationship but it can end at any moment. Their friends will always come first. The image they project to the other students is going to be more important than the relationship they have with you. I may have let the kid down in that situation in a way because of my strong reaction to him, and he may have even only been joking, but to me it was totally inappropriate and reflected what I think is what's getting him into trouble as well here, his just total lack of respect for teachers. Developing relationships and good relationships, where I can get on well with the kids, that gives me a sense of hope and a sense of the future. And when that's broken or damaged in some way, a lot of that trust that's been built up is damaged as well. I'm pretty hard on myself too. I feel as if I could have handled the situation better. Sometimes I overreact or I jump down someone's throat inappropriately or whatever. Sometimes I break that trust that I've built up, they've built up with me, and then all of a sudden they see me acting in a way they may get in their home life and all around, and so they think 'You're just the same as everyone else'.

FRAGILE

SOLD

It's hard to talk about hope with the teachers here. They feel that I'm probably too soft with the kids for a start. They feel that I'm a bit soft with them, and probably nurture them a bit too much. The idea of hopefulness would seem like a soft thing, a soft approach. But hopefulness is important here. I do talk with the kids about hope. I just feel that they need that, and they need a lot more positive in their life, and maybe a little bit more nurturing to get hope. You can only get hope through having that, instead of just playing that strict role of the rules. I just feel there are other ways of dealing with it to get hope. You have to have chance after chance sometimes, to get hope.

Growing up as a child, I didn't have the best upbringing, so I value working with them to try and help them and see their way, before they go through what I went through before I got myself out. Hopefulness means the children, or the kids that I work with, they can succeed without getting into trouble with the law for drugs or whatever. For me personally hope would be that my kids basically succeed, and that I go before them, that they don't go before me. Hope for me is to maybe track some more family that I was taken from: looking for my love for my family.

The most important place here is where the kids are finding it hard in the class and to be around that, to calm them. When a child's got a problem, or is losing it, to be there, and have the challenge of calming them down. If you see they're freaking out in the class, not just to send them, go and talk to them. Just by sitting with them and helping them with their work. Just spending time with them, at recess and lunch, and if you see that they've got a problem, sitting with them. You can build relationships just sitting with them and helping them. That's the most important thing, is the relationship with the child.

It would help a lot more if you could have one-to-one time with the kid, it would build a better relationship a lot faster than if you've got three kids in a class. The kind of place where you could do that might be at the movies, even at McDonald's down the road would be a space where I think would be good. Movies, just going to the beach, parks, and things like that. Places that are about pleasure. And fun for the kids. Because that's how you can get through to them more, using a pleasuring place, that they like and enjoy. More so than in a room. If I can take them down the road or to the park, I can get through to them a lot more, in a pleasuring place. I believe you can get more of a relationship in a pleasuring place.

I come from a modest background. My dad worked in factories. Myself and my husband we've worked hard to achieve a level of comfort. That gives me a great deal of satisfaction coming from a modest background. So when I look around at my home and see the things that I've got, and I see the environment I've created for my children, and I compare that to the environment I came from, I can see a significant change. I'm reminded that things can change for the better. Looking back to my childhood and the childhood that I'm providing for my children, there's a huge chasm, but then as a parent I think it's up to us all to try and ensure that each generation has a better life than the previous one. Change can always occur.

And that translates to working here. We've had kids who literally have no hope because their lives are so narrow, their views are so narrow by the circumstances that they've grown up in, that they can't see outside that, so I think for us to be able to give them an idea, or a glimpse, of what could be out there for them is really important, and I think that's what we all try and do in our own ways. I guess I'd use the word 'potential' to try and make the kids understand, or give them a vision of the fact that they're not limited by their lives at this moment, that there is a future for everyone, and that everyone perhaps needs different levels of intervention or assistance, stick in there.

We had a young guy who was here a few years ago – he and I just clicked, we developed a friendship, you know, adult/child, he didn't have a mother, I took on a real maternal role for him. He was in and out of juvenile justice on a regular basis, and I had a lot of people say to me 'Don't waste your time on him'. Again, we had this connection and he still was stealing cars on a regular basis and would drive them interstate, but he would ring me here at the school, he'd ring and let me know he was OK, from different points around the country. I used to talk to him a lot, and he'd get locked up again, and he would write to me where he'd pour out his heart, so this tough guy exterior hid this young man who was very confused, who couldn't see a future, and I used to just talk to him about the possibilities that were there, that yes, he could get a job. 'I'll never get a job'. 'Well actually you could', you know, we used to talk about how he might do that, and in the end, and I'm happy to say, he got an apprenticeship, and is now a qualified roof plumber, and everyone said he was going to end up in Yatala jail, and the last time I spoke to him he said 'I did go to Yatala, but I went there as a roof plumber'.

I suppose you wouldn't work in a place like this unless you saw some sort of hope for the people that you work with. You need to see that there is hope for the individual kids here, otherwise you wouldn't be working here. There's no staff here that don't want the kids to succeed and do well, and have some sort of goal, to be happy and have their needs fulfilled. And hope is also about changing their lives so that the life that they have currently is not the life that they end up with, that they die with. They're obviously a reflection of their parents, and I see it's our job to give them another side to that, that that's not the way it is, that's not going to work for them in their search for hopefulness. And to help them with that search for hopefulness the most important thing is building relationships.

You go through university as a teacher and you're told consistently you're not the students' friend, you're their teacher, but as far as I'm concerned, working in the environment like this, that's not the case all the time, particularly when you first work with them. You have to do things differently, so you've got to bring yourself down from that teacher level, down to a personal level, a friendly level, to find out basically what makes them tick, and that can be really hard for the kids. It's finding common ground and talking about things that they're interested in. And they need to be able to trust the person that they're working with; to be able to see that they're genuine and that they do have empathy, and they can put themselves into their shoes, and kids are pretty receptive of that. They know when someone's not really genuine. You need to show empathy, the knowing where the students are from, and what they've gone through, and being able to show them some trust and respect. Those things need to happen before the learning.

You need to give empathy and give understanding and give respect, but if you're giving and giving and you don't get anything back, it becomes a place where you probably don't want to be for an extended period of time. But having said that, it depends on what you want back, what you see as worthwhile getting back. It can be really small, it can be just a kid being able to talk to you, without abusing you. Or kids will sometimes give you snapshots into their life, at various times, and you know when kids are telling you more about their life, that they're accepting you and that something is happening there. It's an example that you're on the road to hopefulness with them.

hopefulness, utopias, sustainability: fragments

Simon Robb

We are, at the time of the daydream or of the imagined future, both immersed and detached, witnessing the pleasures of a scene, but also partaking in the pleasures of our own creativity. Being capable of daydreaming is the first prerequisite of hopefulness.

The desire to live, or the feeling that life is worth living, 'this urge to live and to speak', manifests itself in the activity of the imagination, through the speech, the writing, the images of the imagination (Bachelard 1988: 3). The imagination is the constructive space that deals with the absence of hope. The imagination is the faculty that sets thought in motion in a way that inspires the desire to know more, to think more. The imagination 'frees us from immediate images and changes them'; it 'deforms what we perceive' and hence if 'no change, or unexpected fusion of images, there is no imagination; there is no imaginative act' (Bachelard 1988: 1). The imagination works with images, for example, and if an image that is present 'does not make us think of one that is absent, if an image does not determine an abundance—an explosion—of unusual images, then there is no imagination' (Bachelard 1988: 1).

We know therefore that we are in the presence of the imagination when we are in the presence of images that work on us in this way. Images that may work like this are those that are in a state of movement; they are the products of a space that is 'open and elusive' (Bachelard 1988: 1). We take account of the imagination, of the workings of the imagination, when we acknowledge the constellation, 'the torrent of words'; an image unleashes within us, as well as the 'ambiguity, double meanings, metaphors' of those words

(Bachelard 1988: 3). The imagination, as a space where hope can take place, is a space that is dynamic, mobile and, to use a Deleuzian term, in a state of becoming.

Spaces in which we daydream must also be spaces where we feel a sense of security and protection, intermingled with a sense of dreamy pleasure that is both real and unreal. We return to these spaces, drawn on by memory and by a natural attraction to them. Certain spaces appear hopeful because they concentrate 'being within limits that protect' (Bachelard 1994: xxxvi). Being is something that needs to be protected and made safe or, at least, being needs to feel that it is safe, and certain images can help us to imagine that we are safe and secure. The image that perhaps best exemplifies the self protected is the house. It is the space in which we write our inner self; it is the space where the inner self can be mapped, where the inner self can be read. These spaces reappear in daydreams and we are likely to recall them when we are in a position of shelter and protection. Where there is no sense of security, where the home does not bring safety, where the home is a place of menace, fear and violence, then there will be a retardation of the integrating facility of the daydream.

Ordinary hopefulness is experienced in the daydream and can also be experienced through exchanges of kindness that are guided by imagined futures, and through participation in the consumption of signs and objects of global capitalism. All of these forms of hopefulness engender a desire to live and depend on an imagined future generated either from within or without, either for oneself or another.

Imagining future happiness may involve seeing oneself with a new car, travelling down a beautiful country road en-route to a fabulous seaside retreat. It is a daydream. It is hopefulness that can be bought. The idea that hopefulness can be felt through buying certain things is utterly pervasive and depends on the production, distribution and consumption of commercial daydreams. It is not hard to move from here to the idea that hopefulness is dependent on one's ability to purchase and possess the fetish object of one's daydream. In this scenario, where hopefulness is wedded to consumption, hopelessness grows worse with poverty. This we might call the first problem of ordinary hopefulness.

The hopefulness that arises from caring requires a giving up of the self to another and an imagining on behalf of another. This is the hopefulness that binds families and communities together in mutual support. We might also say that this hopefulness depends on an ability to give, receive and repay care; to participate in a gift economy. Put another way, the hopefulness that care brings is only available to those who can participate in the cycle of giving, receiving and repaying. We come here to the second problem of ordinary hopefulness, which is that those who don't know how to give, receive and repay care, and those who can't imagine the future on behalf of another, are shut out from the hopefulness that such a system can bring.

If we want to talk about someone's capacity for hopefulness, we might say that it depends on their ability to imagine, their wealth and status, their ability to give, receive and repay kindness, and their ability to be of service to others. And when speaking of a capacity for hopefulness we are speaking of something like the capacity to go on living, or the capacity to want to live. When there is a deficiency, when the capacity for hope is low, there we find a will not to live, or to live for destruction. This is an area that we might also call the margins of hope, or the ruins of utopian hopefulness.

The ruin is an embodiment of what hope seeks and what it attempts to hide and to make absent, and that is decay, failure, mortality and time. The idea that utopias are constituted in relation to failure, destruction, and waste was taken up by Peter Kraftl (2005), who argued that utopias become generators of knowledge when they are problematic or uncanny. He discussed this idea by taking the example of an uncanny architecture that constructs an ambiguous tension between the home as a place of desired comfort and the home as a site of ruin and haunting.

When the 'unhomely' appears in the home, an experience of the uncanny is the result; a sense of uncertainty about the stability of what was previously stable and certain. When Freud tried to evoke the presence of the uncanny he often returned to the image of someone trying to find their way in a dark room, of someone losing their eyes, of having one's eyes plucked out, trying to see in the dark and returning again to the same object (Royale 2003: 108). If we apply this idea to structures or places of hope, we arrive at an ambiguity between ideas about place, rather than a blueprint for what place should be.

A model for an uncanny idea of place can be found in the work of Christo, and in particular the Wrapped Reichstag of Berlin in 1995. Here there is an uncanny transformation of the totality; something known becomes something both unknown and known at the same time. This transformation of place enacts an opening or invitation to think differently; it becomes a space for the imagination. This transformation of known space is an affirmation for thinking differently. It is utopian in the sense that it enacts a transformation of the totality, not so much in terms of practicalities, but conceptually; the familiar world can change and the known can become something unfamiliar. What we believe to be stable and firm becomes unstable and ambiguous. Spaces of hope, according to this idea, are spaces that evoke an absence, a mystery, something knowable yet elsewhere, something hidden or forgotten. These are the inspirations of the ruin; they are the spaces of hope and they are spaces of imaginative life.

If we want to think of hope as a space, then we might consider a space that is in the process of becoming but never fully materialising, or perhaps a space that is open to possibilities rather than one that is settled. A space like this is not finished; it is permeable but not entirely without form. We might also add that such a space, as an epistemology, is one that must admit a persistent ambiguity; we are speaking of a mystery that exists alongside of the desire to know and processes of knowing. Metaphorically, we are speaking of shadows, ruins, alleyways and occult things existing alongside birth, the open house and the bright sun.

We can speak more broadly of a feeling of homeliness that can be imagined or remembered to be occurring in any space. Bachelard's hopefulness is a feeling that the subject has in isolation, or imagines and remembers on their own. We do not wish to restrict homeliness to an activity that occurs in isolation, but rather to expand this idea to include spaces of connection and interaction with others. We are interested in a shared or mutual sense of homeliness and the spaces in which this occurs. The question then becomes where does the subject imagine or remember experiencing feelings of homeliness (happiness, protection, secrecy).

If we are speaking of homeliness we are also speaking of an uncanniness present alongside or within the home. There is an un-homeliness in all spaces of hope and this is cause both for apprehension and exhilaration. We also might need to talk of an instability between present, past and future, for these are the three times of utopia, and of social sustainability. There is however, a failure in the expectation of the imagination realised that needs to be incorporated into any utopian process. We need to consider this notion of failure in conjunction with the other features noted so far, of the ambiguous and generative relationship between imagination and reality, of the necessity to incorporate the movement of time and the failure of time to move; of the presence of horror, anxiety and fear in the basement of the house and the foundations of utopia.

≈≈≈

UTOPIAS ARE ABOUT THE HOPE FOR A BETTER WORLD and can articulate a complex or simplistic idea of what hopefulness might mean. There is a version of utopianism that articulates a transparent hopefulness, one that is relatively naked and naïve, banal even. Here we might be talking of a utopianism of a happy apocalypse, a utopia where everyone is satisfied and content. This is hope for happiness manifested in its most banal form.

Utopias are never where they are realised, and when they are apparently realised there is a residue of feeling that what was desired is somehow still absent. Likewise, as utopias exist somewhere in the future they can never be fully present; they cannot be where they are (Bloch & Adorno 1988). There are feelings attached to the realisation of utopias, the failure of utopias to realise desires, and the ambiguous relationship between utopian desire and its ruination. These feelings, or the affective charge associated with the utopian imagination, can be understood in the light of what Bloch called 'a melancholy of fulfilment' (Bloch & Adorno 1988: 2). I would suggest that, just as there is a melancholy attached to the utopian imagination, there is also a melancholy attached to any positive social imagining and hence the social imagining that constitutes the work of social sustainability. Likewise it is not simply in the realisation of utopias that there is melancholy, but also in the process itself. Failure and the effect associated with it are always present in the processes and products of the utopian imagination. In the realm of utopian representation, the effect of failure manifests in aesthetics of failure. It is an aesthetics of failure that interestingly enough is positioned as the antithesis of a modernist avant-garde. Here, early twentieth century Italian futurism describes the features of an aesthetics of failure:

> the exotic fascination produced by remoteness in space, the picturesque, the imprecise, rusticity, wild solitude, multicolored disorder, twilight shadows, corrosion, weariness, the soiled traces of the years, the crumbling ruins, mould, the taste of decay, pessimism, suicide ... (Marinetti 1914).

This is an apt description of the affective and aesthetic world that haunts modernity and the utopian imagination. It is also the space of hope in a dystopian world organised around surveillance and transparency.

≈≈≈

Sustainability is menacing to those who cannot think through it. There is a feeling of a responsibility here, not towards sustainability, but against its tyranny. Sustainability is, in its double manifestation, within the grasp of the present and entirely beyond it.

Sustainability needs exhaustion. Exhaustion, the idea of a depletion that cannot be recovered, a fatal exhaustion. This kind of depletion seems to be already present here, in the sense of a blandness, a lack of any vitality, a lack of ambiguity and complexity that is the hallmark of an idea that has life, of an idea that sustains. Sustainability is justice exhausted in the future.

And to answer this question (of what is just) there is a need to link that question to what has gone before and what will come in the future, 'beyond therefore the living present in general' (Derrida 1994: xx). There is a responsibility to the past and to the future when writing of justice, to those lives lost and to come, not just of this embodied, material time. There is a need to learn to live 'neither in life nor death alone' but in all lives lived and to be lived (Derrida 1994: xviii). The question of justice, of how to live is pursued not just in being (presence, ontology, the study of being), but also in its other: the non-material presence, the presence that is not wholly present, the shimmering of things past or to come.

When speaking of sustainable societies, someone is speaking of the society of a never-ending critique. This groundless process of critique, this never ending justice—sustainability cannot live long without it.

Loss of community, and the work that community does to sustain itself, is always and has always been happening. The value of narrative labour is revealed when it manifests this lost thing, manifests the loss of communion, the retreat from this world of those who intimately know communion. In this loss is the creation of community, rather than community's disappearance being the creation of a loss: 'what this community has "lost"—the immanence and the intimacy of communion—is lost only in the sense that such a "loss" is constitutive of "community" itself' (Nancy 1991: 12). There is a necessary time when subject and community fall apart and become nothing to each other. Sustainability needs that time when loss appears.

≈≈≈

SUSTAINABILITY AND HORROR: they go hand in hand and there is, it could be said, a horror lurking, living side by side with sustainability, latent at every turn. It is the stability of the sentence that holds the time of sustainability in place, flowing chronologically, one idea to the next, in forward motion, not returning in an uncanny way. The ground of meaning and the time of meaning become unstuck when the latent thing returns, and that is the horror: the return of that thing that sustainability wants to forget—sustainability trapped in fearful and useless repetition. That's where the monster enters, emerging yet again as something unwanted recalled. Something destructive recalled by uttering its name, the name of sustainability uttered backwards. Sustainability re-animates, in the style of a gothic pursuit of knowledge, both community and its corpse.

Destroying the wealth of the community, the heritage of the work of others, the bonds between people, this too comes from a utopian desire. An act inspired by the desire to turn gold to shit. That's a utopian slogan after Sir Thomas More. That's doing social sustainability.

THE FUTURE IS ALWAYS SOMETHING THAT NEVER ARRIVES and belongs alongside the other un-desconstrucables: 'justice, openness to difference, the wholly other, the marginalised ...' (Derrida 1992: 25). The appeal of the future, as Derrida put it, is the appeal of the other, and it is this appeal that we need to respond to now. This is the responsibility that we have towards the future, both the appeal of otherness, and the doing that allows us to hear that appeal (Cornell 2005: 69).

What is worth saying about the future, or worth representing, are those words and those representations that continue to deconstruct what is meant by 'the future'. Yet at the same time the future is also calling on us 'to act now' on behalf of justice, the need of justice, the need of the marginalised, not so that justice can arrive, finally, or that the marginalised can be central, finally, but so that we can sensitise ourselves to their presence even where they appear to be absent (Cornell 2005: 74).

hope, social intervention and the future

Patrick O'Leary

Reform agendas and social intervention

All of the young people who participated in this research have been targets of the social intervention, most often through child welfare, juvenile justice and special educational programs. Their marginality is both characterised by socioeconomic status and, critically, by social intervention. These interventions have received much critical review for their element of social control while creating traps within the prevailing social conditions (Eheart, Hopping, Power, Mitchell & Racine 2009; Piper 2001). Politically these interventions have been justified not only as way of addressing inequality and social disadvantage, but also as way offering hope to change existing oppressive circumstances towards a desired future (Burnett 2004; Piper 2001).

Often, critiques of young people can dismiss or trivialise their practices in art, fashion, music, sexuality, relationships and, ironically, their aspirations. Within mainstream society, young people's expression of graffiti, body art and fluidity in relationships and identity is seen as problematical and a target of correction (Burnett 2004). These cultural expressions can be a positive resistance to the norm and consequentially a demonstration of hope for difference and change. Much of the burden of intervention falls on young people that are on the margins of society (Burnett 2004). This group of young people is relatively a easy target for pessimism and is consequently the target of social reform (Piper 2001). This strategy, underpinned by political law and order campaigns to correct the social morals of young people, is often characterised by punishment and training methods such as boot camps where military style discipline is seen as the antidote.

In 1972, Cohen examined the construction of deviance among the youth culture of that time and the resulting moral panic that supported intervention to exert social control. In contemporary times, media and political law and order campaigns have fed this moral panic, leading to increased attention on punishment and correction regimes (Welch, Price &Yankey 2000). Much of this intervention has been strongly biased towards lower social classes and non-white groups. These interventions have been critiqued because their rhetoric has been liberating, when first and foremost social control has been the primary purpose (Johansson 2000).

Aetiology, correction and narrative therapy

Social intervention and research on young people on the margins has been strongly influenced by these social and political agendas. This has seen a particular orientation towards correctional and etiological (cause) based research questions (Raaijmakers, Engels & Van Hoof 2005). Research has been geared towards finding the cause of problems such as deviancy, delinquency and criminality. Corresponding responses are oriented towards returning these young people to normative social behaviour and participation

(Welsh, Price & Yankey 2005). In turn this has shaped some assumptions about the morals and views of young people as they move in a global society that is becoming increasingly less environmentally, economically, politically and socially sustainable. While the possibilities of the future have been expanded as a result of the rapid expansion in global, technological and information environments, the risks for sustainability and a civil society have also increased. This has raised more questions about the preparedness of young people to enter an uncertain and insecure world.

Although the participation of these young people in mainstream opportunities is a worthwhile pursuit, we need to be careful about assumptions that young people on the margins have different or non-desirable aspirations for the future, and as a result we need to better identify common hope. Braithwaite (2004) highlighted the tensions of presenting hope that is reasonably attainable within the balance of support and resources that create dependence, passivity and ultimately hopelessness. Programs that offer support and resources without empowerment tend to trap young people in the hopelessness of dependence. On the other hand, programs that engage in the psychology of creating hope without support and resources to effect structural change in the distribution of resources, can result in a failure to realise and materialise hope. As Braithwaite (2004a: 87) highlighted:

> Hope is not only important at the commanding heights but also vital for any underclass that seeks to throw off the shackles that persist in holding it down.

Friere (1994) proposed that hope is essential for marginalised people to be able to offer resistance that brings about change and difference:

> Without a minimum of hope, we cannot so much as start the struggle. But with the struggle, hope, as an ontological need, dissipates, loses its bearings, and turns into hopelessness. (Freire 1994: 2)

To try and capture young people's resistance and alternative stories, we employed the research methods of narrative therapy. The underlying assumption of this approach is that people have multiple stories, and the meaning attached to these stories can be central to how the past, present and future are viewed and enacted. What seems to be an overtly dystopian standpoint of hope and the future, needs to be understood in relation to the past and present; consequently there maybe paradoxical meanings. With the category of 'delinquent', a dominant storyline is played out, but often underlying this there is a competing story that is alternative and more aligned to one's self agency and preferred identity. Parts of this competing version of identity often offer a resistance to the dominant storyline. For many of the young people in this research, the dominant storyline was inherently negative and based on deficit or pathology.

A narrative approach draws together both individual and collective perspective on what constitutes individual and community lives at a socio-political level. It is both paradoxical and subversive in its positioning of people and communities experiencing hardship. In this way it locates problems as separate from identities, rather than manifestations of the individual or community. Narrative therapy places particular importance on justice and resistance to oppression by attempting to ask what is preferred for future ways of being. This is called re-authoring, a way of challenging some stories that have been created, internalised and reinforced by pathology, and locating problems as deficits contained in the marginalised individual or group (White & Epstein 1990).

> And there are persons who are endeavouring to situate their lives in preferred stories and to embrace alternative knowledges, but who are finding it difficult to do so because of the dominant and disqualifying stories or knowledges that others have about them and their relationships (White & Epstein 1990: 76).

As a response, narrative therapy advocates a non-authoritarian approach that positions the individual or community as the expert of their lives. Through this approach, not only personal agency, but also the socio-political context of people's lives are the target of intervention. By appreciating people's history of struggle, there can be a potential to establish conditions that facilitate the performance and circulation of hopes and preferred futures. The approach allowed the research for this book to explore not only the likely futures that were attached to the category of marginalised, but also, by placing young people at the centre of the inquiry, they could become authors of hope and a desired or preferred future.

> The narrative mode locates a person as a protagonist or participant in his/her world. This is a world of interpretative acts, a world in which every retelling of story is a new telling, a world in which a person participates with others in the 're-authoring' and thus in the shaping, of their lives and relationships (White & Epstein 1990: 82).

Young people's stories

Although we did not ask specifically whether the young people had, for example, been a victim of abuse or violence, it was quickly evident that the majority of young people had experienced significant and often ongoing upheaval and trauma. Many of them had been the subject of child welfare intervention, and several remained under the guardianship of the state. For example, one young man constructed his desired future in juxtaposition to his experience of childhood:

> in twenty years hopefully I am a builder with a child who won't have a drug addict father or mother ... no trouble or hiding ... he will have freedom... he will have the comfort of his family around... I want to have an everyday life...

It was not uncommon for young people to reveal many changes of residence and school, while others reported multiple foster care placements during their young lives. These social histories point to recurring family separation and exile. Many of the young people had a long history of statutory relationships with social institutions such as child welfare. Research on juvenile detention institutions and behaviour units outside mainstream schooling institutions show an over representation of young people with abuse and child welfare histories (Mistral & Evans 2002).

Young people often gave the researchers snippets of their anger and frustration with family members and professionals for past and present injustices. The complexity of these feelings was related to the fact that, in some instances, these same people were relied on for support and resources. In other instances, anger and revenge were motivations to punish or prove others wrong in the future. A testament to the resilience of many of the young people was an enduring hope for selected family and friends, even when there had been a problematic history of support and connection. This is of particular relevance to Synder's (2002) hope theory that asserts that hope develops best in environments of secure and supportive relationships with adults. The importance of relationships for survival and hope was regularly evident from our interviews with the young people. In the following quote, a young man reflects on hope and his relationship with his mother. He recalls how despite being in jail his mum is who he most wants to be in with in the future:

> If I could imagine being with anyone it would be my mum. She makes me feel safe. She knows what to say. She's always been there. Unless she's in jail.

Synder's (2002) theory on hope also highlights the importance of instilling confidence to allow one to cognitively and purposefully plan for the future. One young man talked about a teacher who had given him confidence to plan and be hopeful about the future:

> There's a teacher who thinks I could do anything I want to do. He's the one who got me into my last TAFE course which was an introduction to animal care, which I passed … I'll probably have a couple pets of my own.

Different, but not unrelated to experiences of injustice, are the actions of the young people that had resulted in criminal convictions. Many of the young men had been involved in violence, theft and vandalism. Others without criminal convictions described antisocial behaviour, failure to attend school and other violations of school rules. Unsolicited explanations of these actions revealed a range of intentions from a desire to do harm, through to a defiance or resistance to institutions. Stealing a car and being pursued by the police, for example, was explained as a way of getting a rush or excitement, relieving boredom or increasing peer status. In other cases, anarchy in social groups was a reaction to societal restraints and expectations.

Images of violence, crime, and risk taking, as well as statements that revealed violent intentions such as bashing people, were also part of the young men's engagement with some of the more violent extremes of hegemonic masculinity. There has been interest more recently in the construction of masculinity in marginalised groups of males, including the following groups: non-heterosexual, non-white, working class, lower socio-economic, young, and incarcerated males. In groups of incarcerated and socially disadvantaged males, various writers have observed that masculinity can be exaggerated to some of its worst extremes 'to make visible a gender order that encourages boys to pursue the shared enterprise of hyper-masculinity making, characterised by physical domination, aggression and competitive 'macho' bravado that denigrates females and anything considered feminine' (Smith 2007: 184). It was emphasised by Connell (2000) that such practices are particularly concentrated in institutions and regimes that assert control or correction. These often lead to what Connell described as complicit masculinities, a way fitting in or being normalised in social practices.

It was evident in the interviews that some young men need to demonstrate masculine creditability by telling stories of dominant masculine traits or feats of the past. In most cases, the stories emphasised power through the use of or threat of violence, or the display of heterosexual practices with desirable or stereotypical ideas of femininity and sexuality. For example, one young man described past acts of violence against police when he had been arrested, while another said 'I can see myself with a hot missus'. In both cases these 'tellings' were strategic in that they presented a track record or desire of masculine identity that was acceptable and credible in terms of power. There was not necessarily an assertion of intent, rather the potential to use power seemed important. For example, one young man's photo of ceremonial knives was described as one of power rather than enactment of violence. In the expression of violence towards others was vengeance based on experiences of injustice; a kind of principle stand or justification.

Alternatives to the hopes of hegemonic and complicit masculinity often featured the hopes of family and connection to significant others. Young men were reluct to assume exploitive, violent or irresponsible masculine practices mostly because they had been victimised by these exact practices. For example, one young man reflected on his surviving a household in which violence was a regular occurrence:

> My mum and my mates and some cops would know how tough things have been for me ... when shit used to happen they'd come round and help me out.

Part of presenting a different masculinity was the hope to be different from adult men in their lives, such as future hopes to be a father:

> I wouldn't mind being a Dad. But I'd want to better than my Dad.

These stories do not paint young people on the margins as passive victims. Their actions reveal transitions between roles of positive defiance as well as the oppressor and oppressed. Most of the representations of masculinity can be sourced from culture and media portrayals, similarly dystopian viewpoints also are often not esoteric creations, but are often part of the broader experience of socially excluded communities and an increasingly insecure world.

Where do the dystopian and non-desirable futures come from?

The futures described by the young people that cause us concern are disturbing, but they are not new to present day society. These images and narratives are stories that reveal societal fears. They are part of the justifications for both etiological and correctional based responses. At the same time, these are outcomes readily available in popular media and regularly experienced in socially excluded communities. Depictions of a life committing crime and establishing a family while in jail are not just dystopias, but realities when we look at the social background of the inmates of today's prisons. Recreational use of alcohol and illegal drugs is already an accepted mode of social enjoyment and culture. Generational unemployment and substance dependence are significant and widespread social problems. Having weapons as source of power, deterrence and status is not unfamiliar to the storylines of television and the daily news. The dystopias presented by young people are as much a societal creation as the desired futures of wealth, large houses and fast cars. These dystopian ideas must be seen in the context of current experience.

Some dystopian representations are on the surface, concerning, but they may paradoxically offer some counter plot and resistance to the mainstream. Where this is the case we might circumvent exciting propositions for change that are not in our consciousness and that may have the potential to create a sustainable and positive future. This is not to discount our fears and concerns as being legitimate or unwarranted, but rather advocate for openness and critical appraisal of what hope is and what it is in response to. To do this requires us to critically use what we already know about the stratification and effect of marginalisation and its relationship with a hopeful future social intervention also needs to go beyond cause and correctional response paradigms.

The stories in this book reveal a strong alliance between mainstream and marginal conceptions of hope. Essentially, young people have expressed the need to find a place in the world where they have intimate connections with family and friends, and the luxuries of technology and wealth to create comfort and excitement. These hopes are likely to strike a chord with most people. Furthermore, we all share a need to be cared for, valued and noticed in our communities. The less desirable presentations of hope and the future have, on the one hand, created a counter plot or resistance to taken for granted hopes for the future, while on the other hand they merely resemble chronic conditions that are already present for socially excluded people. Young people's stories offer some insight into less desirable versions of hope and the future, as well as demonstrating the strong resilience required to hold on to hope for the future.

Conclusions: what institutions of hope are available to young people on the margins?

Having traversed the complexities of hope among young people on the margins, what can we take away from this book? Young people's experience of both their social conditions and resulting intervention best capture responses that are not helpful. Longstanding and chronic social conditions left important relationships strained and impoverished. Images and words of young people capture the way marginalisation at personal and institutional levels can occur, as one young man reflected on visit to his mother:

> On my birthday my mother was supposed to give me $100 but instead she spent it on alcohol and the pokies. But I didn't ask her about it because she'd lost her best friend. He was like my second Dad. I didn't accept what she did but I understood why she did it.

On the other hand, the response of state care and intervention often artificially produced relationships that were difficult to sustain with meaning and connection. The same young man recounted his current living conditions under the guardianship of the state, away from the chaos and poverty of his family:

> I live in a motel where a carer is paid to look after me. A different carer comes on every eight hours.

These two accounts demonstrate how family relationships can be painful and fragile, while the intervention lacks sustainable connection or meaningful space. These observations reverberate strongly with other themes explored in this book: namely the importance of respect (Alison Mackinnon), caring for hope (Peter Bishop) and having spaces of security and protection where dreams can be cultivated (Simon Robb). All of these offer suggestions on how to orient education and social intervention towards hope. It also highlights the power of engaging with young people's experience and struggle as a starting point for creating positive change.

The challenge with reorienting responses to young people is that there is not an immediate or specific design that can be directly translated, for example, to a reduction in juvenile crime or youth unemployment. Intervention needs be seen as a community responsibility where there is a belief in everyone's capacity to care (Elheart et al. 2009: 52). In this way institutions need to consider practices that provide space, transition and connection, in addition to practices measured by outcomes of qualification, employment or low recidivism. It seems that for some young people, these desirable outcomes are more difficult to attain without a background or foundation in stable and safe experiences. Braithwaite (2004b: 7) suggested:

> Institutions of hope refer to sets of rules, norms, and practices that ensure we have some room not only to dream of the extraordinary but also to do the extraordinary.

This type of institution challenges or at least offsets constraints imposed by regulatory institutions. Of course the challenge to create such institutions is extended to society at a general level, and to its response to young people on the margins. This is not to say that order and structure to guide young people to sustainable and active lives is not essential for a civil society. Rather the former is not possible without meaningful relationships, with care and respect accorded to people's hopes and dreams, no matter how embryonic.

If there is a fundamental message in this book, it is that there is a need to ask young people what they draw hope from, and what they hope for in the future, in a way that allows them to present their other stories. This needs to be aligned to a substantial hope that acts with purpose and resolve. A place that demonstrates this resolve is the presentation of experience and imagination in a way that cultivates hope with sensibility (Shearing & Kempa 2004). This book and the 2008 museum exhibition (Robb, Mackinnon, Bishop, O'Leary & Hart 2008) are some of the first steps that attempt to enact this practice. Schools and institutions that support young people might consider reflexive approaches to purpose and freedom along the lines that hooks (1994: 12) suggested:

> I celebrate teaching that enables transgressions—a movement against and beyond boundaries. It is that movement which makes education the practice of freedom.

respect, risk and relatedness

Alison Mackinnon

Respect

As we walk into one of the schools we visited in the project, the slogan 'Respect, Responsibility, Resilience' greets us. It is on the wall, on the notice boards, all around us. How much respect do young people on the margins receive and where do they receive it? I consider respect to be one of the three 'Rs' for creating hopeful futures, part of what Victoria McGeer called 'the parental and peer scaffolding' which nurtures hope (McGeer 2004: 193ff). Respect is hard to come by in our society. As Richard Sennet pointed out, when a society only singles out a few for recognition, 'it creates a scarcity of respect' (Sennett 2003: 3). The need for respect has become a mantra, the British government has for example, made it a catchcry in their policy for their disaffected young 'hoodies'. They even instituted a Respect Task Force.

Our participants often mentioned the issue of respect. One young man told us: 'You've got to give them some respect to get respect from them. If you want to get treated well, treat them well. I feel respected here'. Another at that school claimed:

> I feel respected by the staff. You've got more leeway than in a normal school. Heaps more leeway than in a normal school. If you're in a bad mood they give you more leeway. They tell you positive things. They tell you what will happen if you do good. They tell you what you can achieve.

A troubled young man, struggling with his anger (understandable, perhaps, when one hears about his background) said: 'Sometimes I go off the deep end a bit. People staring at me makes me angry. I'd just like people's respect. The police make me angry. The very presence of them makes me furious'. But this young man too feels accepted in this particularly effective small alternative educational setting: 'I feel respected here', he told us, 'more respected than in other schools. They see I'm trying. They respect me a lot more for it. I show them respect too'. One young woman felt the lack of respect as a real barrier:

> Interviewer: So there have been people that you feel haven't respected you in your life?
>
> Young woman: Oh yeah.
>
> Interviewer: At school?
>
> Young woman: There's a lot of them.

Teachers too struggled with trying to give the young people respect and care:

> and sometimes you'll have some hard-nut kid that's come into your class, and you treat them with respect, and you treat them like a normal person, you speak to them like a normal person, and then they're angels … You've really got to try and not judge the students, and when you do take them as normal individuals, and treat them like normal human beings, like probably a lot of other people haven't, that's when I find that you will be able to teach them, because they, they'll listen, and then they'll respect you as well, and then when they respect you, then you can actually start to teach them things …

Respect is a reciprocal matter—you give some, you get some. But very often no-one is prepared to make the first move. At schools which aim to create a hopeful atmosphere for disturbed or troubled young people it is essential that staff make the first move. As one teacher remarked, 'Hopefulness is created in relationships between teacher and student when the teacher is empathetic, friendly, respectful and genuine'.

Our goal was to ascertain what gave young people a sense of hope, as we have seen, of hopefulness in the future. Not surprisingly we found that most young people, even those who might be perceived as being on the margins, aspired to the same goals as the rest of us: a good job, a family, a house and car—perhaps some of the luxuries of life. 'In twenty years time I can see myself with my own house, sitting on the couch and watching TV. Maybe kids. I want a car too. I'd want my kids to be good people. I'd want my kids to be strong and shit so they can stick up for themselves like I've had to stick up for myself', claimed one of our young people. They were both 'normal' teenagers in their desires and at the same time different due to the difficult circumstances they faced.

Risk

We live in a risk society, we are told (Beck 1992). Yet the term 'risk' is often used derogatively of young people. The young people whose hopes we shared are often described as being 'at risk'. What is meant by the designation 'at risk'? Is the application of the term 'at risk' to certain groups of young people an admission of society's failure to accommodate them in modern social structures? Does the notion of 'at risk' signify a particular life stage for some young people who cannot acquire the material goods they aspire to in a consumer saturated society? Does it suggest an institutionalised anxiety about young people who appear to be different in appearance and values?

Clearly uncertainty, change and insecurity are part of the modern global economy. Some argue that risk may be the defining concept of the 21st century. Innovators are urged to take risks. Entrepreneurs often embody the benefits of risk taking and were, until recently, praised for it. We encourage young people to be enterprising. Is some of the global risk projected onto vulnerable young people whose life chances are severely limited? We prefer the term 'marginalised' for young people to indicate something deficient in the relationship (with school, with work) rather than the implied implication of deficiencies in the students themselves that the term 'at risk' brings with it.

Yet there is another side to risk. Risk is exciting, thrilling; it offers a release from the boredom of unfulfilled lives. Young people, young men in particular, enjoy speed and pitting themselves against challenging obstacles. They like to drive fast. Young people who may not have access to the socially sanctioned sources of risk are adept at finding some for themselves. Illicit drugs, stolen cars and police chases, deviant behaviours, the possession and use of weapons—all offer a world of risk and adrenalin rushes, of escape from hopelessness. Hopefulness inheres in that escape.

How can we provide some of that excitement for young people through schools and associated activities in ways that do not expose them to the juvenile justice system? Providing socially sanctioned means of risky behaviour is another building block of hope. Through challenging themselves young people learn to respect themselves and gain the respect of peers.

Relatedness

Teachers and counsellors were clear that the way to establish hopefulness was through building relationships with young people. Those relationships varied from maternal to that of a mentor or of a friend. 'The only way it works here is the power of your relationships', said one. This perhaps is the most important of the keys to building hope.

Another pointed out the need to persist in building relations with young people, 'You have to have chance after chance sometimes, to get hope'.

That persistence in the face of discouragement from others was demonstrated by the youth worker who told the following story:

> We developed a friendship ... I took on a real maternal role for him ... I had a lot of people say to me 'Don't waste your time on him'. He still was stealing cars on a regular basis and would drive them interstate, but he would ring me here at the school, he'd ring and let me know he was OK ... I used to talk to him a lot, and he'd get locked up again, and he would write to me where he'd pour out his heart ... and I used to just talk to him about the possibilities that were there, that yes, he could get a job ... and I'm happy to say, he got an apprenticeship, and is now a qualified roof plumber ...

Educator David Halpin argued persuasively that hopefulness entails both anticipating future happiness and 'trusting in present help to come to it' (Halpin 2003). The small story above makes that point superbly: the help did come and was persistent, where others might have given up. Halpin believed that mutuality is 'both a source for, and a potential outcome of, hope. It is also closely bound up with the willingness to experiment, to make choices, and to be adventurous'. Accordingly, he continued, 'hope has a creative role in encouraging the development of imaginative solutions to seemingly intractable difficulties' (Halpin 2003).

YOUR

Some adults too are willing to experiment, to make choices, to be adventurous. Here one teacher describes a willingness to treat young people with difficulties as a friend.

> Maintaining relationships with the kids is just like you do with any friend … you treat the kids like friends. You take an interest in your friends, you enquire after them, and you remember their birthdays, you remember the names of their siblings, and their mothers and fathers, and if you don't see them for a while and you catch up 'Oh, how's your mother going?' knowing that X's mother had been locked up for drug offences, and has been released, or saying 'Do you need any food? We put a food parcel together for you to take home. How are you going?' … It's about just being a genuine friend to them …

Some adults working with young people know only too well from personal experience how important that sense of friendship is, that ability to stay the course:

> I had always been intent on doing harm to myself and not wanting to live, but I reached a point where I thought I want to be happy and enjoy my life. My family, who are incredibly supportive, and a few close friends that I have thought that I would never even make it to the age I am. And they look at me now and just say 'Wow!' you have come so far, and I have, I really have. I guess I always knew that they believed in me, and that's important I think, if there's someone that can say to you 'You're OK, and I believe in you, I have faith, I'm here for you'.

Those who work with young people on the margins need a strong sense of hope and a capacity to put themself in another's place. 'Even when things are going rough', a teacher told us, 'at the back of your mind you know that if you keep supporting them, you keep showing them the right path, if you keep being a mentor, and walk for a moment in their shoes as well … that holds you in good stead'.

On Hollywood Boulevard: which way to the future?

Where does 'walking in the shoes of the young women in the project take us? One of our young women photographed a place with a highly evocative name emblematic of both her hopes and fears: 'Hollywood Boulevard', a real place in her neighbourhood, provides a poignant reminder of the gulf between hope and reality, between the worlds of everyday life, popular culture, the celebrity and utopian dreams of a world beyond the ordinary. How close would the lives of the young women in the project get to Hollywood? In this age of Big Brother and celebrity makeovers, everyone can hit the jackpot, be transported to another more exciting world in a flash. Is the future in their hands or is it all just a stroke of fate?

Any sense of individualism our young women portrayed was overridden by a sense of connectedness more important than individual quest. Individual desires were there, nevertheless. One girl, for instance, wanted to travel, to escape and maybe find a future—not 'take any shit from anyone'.

> I'd prefer to be working so I could save up, like you know, I'm only 14, I've got to wait until I'm 15 at least so I can go and get a job ... saving some money, and this is the place that can help me get a job, so this is the place I want in my future, so it can help me get a job, so in the future I can get a job so I can go.

Yet as well as this assertion of independence, the girl is bound by a sense of fate, of 'the cards you are dealt' as this exchange reveals:

> Researcher: There have been some tough times?
>
> Girl: Yeah, but like everybody you get over it and move on, deal with the cards you get dealt. [And later] But I talk about, I mean most of the time just like, yeah, well these are the cards I've been dealt, that's what I've got to do ... and ... when ... you just feel yourself going downhill and I just get in a real shit with everyone, and I mean that's what I mean. I don't really know how I get myself out of them because like, yeah, it just happens.
>
> Researcher: Do you ... notice anything about your hopes for the future that you see particularly unique to you, from what you hear other kids talk about, or other young people talk about?
>
> Girl: Yeah ... most people, like people I hang around with are just like 'Yeah, whatever happens, happens, just deal with it as it comes', so I don't really know if I see myself like that far in the future.

'Whatever happens, happens: deal with it as it comes', what does this apparent fatalism tell us about these young women and their sense of the future? Their lives, when they do reflect on them, do not show the hallmarks of the individualising biographical project much remarked on by recent sociologists, but rather lives of connection and of helping others, whose difficulties they know all too well. Girls too like having fun together.

Possibly the most obvious purveyor of dreams is popular culture. The girls' photos are redolent of popular culture. They pose for each other with pouting lips, hips thrust forward, midriffs fashionably bare, often in groups. They look both sexy and playful, tempting, perhaps, an element of danger. They are both playing at being sexual and being sexy, although not always for the audiences we might imagine. Their poses are not original but echo those of many young women whose YouTube entries and video clips they emulate, the stars of our celebrity world. Their bedrooms, havens and places of secret gatherings, are adorned with posters of their favourites.

They hope too for relatedness, for families, for parents who care, for 'friendly people that all have lives and have jobs and that will go to work every weekday'. They love to care for others, for little nieces and nephews, for pets, for friends, and maybe for parents whose lives are off the rails. A house, a family, jobs and everyday life—that is paradise indeed, while at the same time it is possible to dream one day of walking the real Hollywood Boulevard—if those are the cards you are dealt.

Building institutions of hope and the usefulness of hope

I have been talking in the main of the need to build hope in young people through giving them respect, through providing acceptable risk taking opportunities and through relatedness. By so doing we prepare them to play an active part in civil society, to be socially included and to be part of a sustainable society. This is itself critically important. Psychologists remind us that hoping well underpins an ability to act in society (McGeer 2004), 'to take a reflective and developmental stance towards our own abilities'. Political philosopher Phillip Pettit argued that hope is a cognitive counterpart of planning while John Braithwaite argued that 'high hope people' can overcome helplessness by being better able to conceptualise their goals (Hope, Power and Governance 2004).

But can we go further and build a collective sense of hope, build institutions of hope that will further strengthen the young people whose hopes we have seen? In an interesting collection of writing which aims *inter alia* to establish the principles of institutions of hope, we can begin to see a way of moving productively from individual hope to a more collective form. Valerie Braithwaite pointed out that 'here institutions of hope refer to sets of rules, norms and practices that ensure that we have some room not only to dream of the extraordinary but also to do the extraordinary' (Braithwaite 2004: 7). Or perhaps the ordinary? As we have seen, many of the hopes and dreams of the young people featured here are of the ordinary rather than the extraordinary, but the same principles apply. She also noted that 'probably the two most important allies of hope realization are empowerment and action'. It is important in this scheme of things that hope is also accompanied by some planning and analysis.

How can hope be put into action for young people who experience the multiple disadvantages of poverty? John Braithwaite (2004a) believed that a more effective route is through a reciprocal building of emancipation from hope and hope from emancipation. Here indeed hope is allied to planning. Braithwaite outlined a Californian program, 'The Emancipation Conference', which sets out to move young people from foster care to independent living. In each 'conference' the young person sets an agenda and includes five of his or her strengths. They invite people they want for help and support to attend. The facilitator of the conference is trained to focus on strength building, not on problems. The discussion that follows considers how strengths can be used to achieve goals. The young person then writes an emancipation plan. Others at the conference help to strengthen it and offer support. Finally timelines are agreed on and a follow up conference is scheduled. This sketchy outline is of course only part of the story. As Braithwaite said, hope is built with plans, resources and support. Other parts of the program teach independent living skills and provide scholarships.

Yet it does offer a way forward in building on hope, on being able not only to see a future, a difficult task for some young people, but being able to actively plan for a future. It draws on people who the young persons respect and who are in a relationship with them, developing trust.

Where secondary school students are routinely expected to formulate Personal Learning Plans (such as in the new South Australian Certificate of Education SACE), an expectation of hope for the future is inbuilt, taken for granted. An understanding of the importance of 'hoping well' is vital for the success of such plans. As the advice to students points out 'The Personal Learning Plan is all about thinking seriously about your future, and planning for that future' (SACE 2009). In this context it is even more important for students from the margins who may not take for granted a future as we have seen, to have their hopes recognised and understood—and respected.

caring for hope

Peter Bishop

There are many reasons why people hope or at least try to find hope. Similarly there are many things for which people hope. People from all cultures, backgrounds, ages and times seem to hope. As such it is a fundamental human experience. While the internal psycho-dynamics of hope are probably constant through the ages, the experiences and the contours of hope must vary considerably according to circumstances. As a focus for research, hope is generally linked to some larger project. It could be part of teaching and education, for example. Hope then becomes integral to better, richer, more dynamic teaching and learning. Alternatively, hope can be evoked in a context of healing, whether therapeutic or spiritual. Hope is also crucial to social change, to the imagining of and struggle for a better society.

Certainly in the background of this research project there were questions about hope as part of questions about a sustainable culture, particularly as experienced from the margins of contemporary mainstream Australian society. It also linked hope to what could be called a utopian imagination, one that provides glimpses, sparks, fragments of hybrid, in-between spaces, of openings to better possibilities.

But, while this research was connected to big discussions about a sustainable society, our main concern was with an everyday kind of hope. Above all, we wanted to listen to the expressions of hope rather than rushing in to interpret their meaning, to impose our frameworks, or our own requirements onto images and ideas that were often quite tentative and personal. As researchers, we recognised that we had a responsibility of care towards the process. Encouraging people to explore their hopes is not something to be treated carelessly.

Hope is generally directed towards dissatisfaction with the present state of affairs and some desired improvement in a person's life. It can expose fragility, perhaps a weakness. For many people this admission can expose vulnerabilities, both to others and to themselves. Hope can invoke fear, insecurity, and unrealistic expectations. There can be suspicion of hope and of expectation; a fear of false hope. There is something unsettling and disturbing about hoping. It can introduce turbulence where there was previously resignation or stoicism.

Hoping can therefore sometimes involve risk, but it can also keep us going, encourage us to try to change things and help build confidence. Hope is therefore double-edged. No wonder that it was one of the evils locked away in the Pandora's Box of Greek mythology, a curse for humanity as well as a boon.

People find hope, are given hope, build hope and steal hope. There are people, places and things that bring hope. But, however hope is attained, an affective dimension generally accompanies it, an emotional investment (Zembylas 2005: 95). To intrude on this terrain of emotions and fantasies needs careful consideration. This is especially the case when people who are asked to express their hopes are both young and marginalised in finance and education, and in advancement opportunities in mainstream society. Hope from such a social position is not always easy, nor is it always readily accessible. It could be called difficult hope. Encouraging people, often in positions of vulnerability, to turn their attention in such a complex and sensitive direction needs care.

Researching hope involves three key processes. First it requires hope to be elicited, evoked and encouraged, or to be at least contemplated as a possibility. Second it requires hope to be recognised, no matter how ephemeral or even strange it may at first appear, no matter how fleeting or seemingly distant from everyday circumstances. Finally these manifestations of hope have to be handled and worked, presented in some way and read, commented on, perhaps even understood.

Hope and the researcher

When discussing social research, the sociologist John O'Neill insisted that 'We begin in the midst of things' (1975: 1). The lives of these young people are already rich, complex and well-established when we enter for just a brief moment of intersection. He suggested that research begins, 'at home in the world of familiar objects, among friends and everyday scenes' (1975: 2). I want to draw on O'Neill's seminal work because it maps out a form of enquiry that is not only deeply respectful of the world it is investigating, but is also critically reflexive about the limitations of the researcher. It is an approach of care and concern which is appropriate for researching a difficult and often fragile hope. O'Neill suggested that 'we need to cultivate what is near to us', because 'we make our lives from what is around us, from our family, our house, street ... friends' (1975: 9). The images in this book testify that this was certainly the case with these young people, our collaborators, and the experiences and images of hope that they revealed to us, although there were also other more offbeat images of hope, surreal fantasies and unhomely, abandoned places.

The research also involved our hopes, both the expectations and desires for the research to succeed, and our hopes for these young people. Also, this research threw another light onto our own, personal hopes, exposing, for example, our position in the social matrix, with its assumptions, agendas and presuppositions. This kind of work challenges the capacity to care for the hopes of another. It inevitably involves an interaction between feeling, thinking, intuition and sensing, both for those called on to express their hopes and, importantly, for the researcher. Care had to be taken not to transfer or project our own hopes (or hopelessness and frustrations) onto those being expressed by our young research collaborators. Attention to such issues is crucial when working with such affective dimensions, where complex emotions quietly infuse the whole project.

The rituals of approach

ALL SENSITIVE RESEARCH requires 'moving into the lives of others, interrupting their thoughts, or getting them to pause on their way, or to set aside their work for a moment. For these reasons we need to trust to the rituals of approach even where, as sometimes happens, they do not quite succeed' (O'Neill 1975: 70).

Every society has its own world of hope and hoping. The dimensions of hope, its forms and expressions are understood and shared by members of society. In Michael Oakeshott's evocative phrase, societies are a kind of conversation, and as such there is a social conversation around hope (O'Neill 1975: 17). Marginality can mean that it is difficult to participate in,

HOLLYWOOD BVD

let alone contribute to, such a conversation. The natural assumptions about expectations, about resources that are available, the language used in the conversation, the tone of the conversation can all contribute to marginalisation, even exclusion. As Oakeshott pointed out, 'an initiation into the skill and partnership of this conversation' is crucial for all members of a society (1962: 199). This research is, in some small way, an attempt to make the conversation about hope more inclusive.

A care for language

'A care for language shapes our responsibility to ourselves and others' (O'Neill 1975: 18). This care begins with our attempts to turn people's attention towards hope. With the invitation to hope and the elicitation of hope, issues of trust are always close to the surface. A care for language continues with sensitivity towards hope, towards recognising it. This demands educated and empathetic listening. What does hope look like? Expressions of hope can seem quite simple, even trivial. One person's hope can be another's platitude.

There needs to be vigilance towards moments of hope and, beyond this, an attention to the rich diversity, complexities, intricacies and depth of an imagination of hope, of pathways by which hope can be accessed and mobilised, plus a care towards the ways in which these are manifest in words and images. As Zembylas pointed out, metaphor and metaphorical language are important in emotional expression and communication (2005: 136). This kind of language requires considered attention. Directness of interpretation is rarely possible and seldom desirable.

Above all, care needs to be exercised when taking these expressions of hope from their personal settings and inserting them into other contexts such as this book. This requirement for care extends into the way we write about these expressions of hope. Hopefulness is a complex, open-ended imaginative process, often serendipitous, difficult and winding. These pathways of hopefulness, with the often intimate affective relationships that people have with them, should not be interrogated, judged, or squeezed into pre-existing frames and categories. On the contrary, perhaps they can make us think again by challenging our assumptions. O'Neill warned against 'an impatient reduction of circumstance to environment, organization, class, and ethnicity' (1975: 26–7). We needed to constantly remind ourselves that we were not studying these young people. The research was not about them. Their expressions of hope did not need to be personally analysed. They were collaborators in our attempts to gain another perspective on hope, one that is seldom seen. The perspective of treating at-risk youth as research collaborators is not easy to sustain. There are strong pressures to objectify and to judge such youth, to analyse them through various disciplinary frames, or to reify them as rebels, or to view them as problems in need of correction. This was not our intent.

O'Neill's insistence that: 'We begin in the midst of things' (1975: 1) doesn't just refer to everyday life, it also applies to the complex weave of theories, perspectives, and social agendas that constitute the world of research. A vital but fleeting and fragile intimation of hope can easily be dismissed by scholarly, critical interrogation and evaluation, or be crushed beneath the weight of social indictments.

While carefully looking at the images and texts produced by the young people I began to think that not all of these showed hope as such. While some could be interpreted in this way, others seemed to express just a general hopefulness, a remembering that hope could be a possibility, perhaps even a desire to hope, an intention to seek hope. I thought that some revealed just a trace, a footprint of a hope.

A care for language also means being true to the tone, to the way that hope is articulated. Many of the young people's representations of hope were couched in a direct, straightforward and sincere style, especially those that expressed an aspiration: 'I want to be a hairdresser'; 'I want two to three kids in the future'; 'I hope to have the friends I have and to get more'; 'hopefulness is having a new car in the future'; 'feeling hopeful is about having lots of money and having that money in cash with you wherever you go'. Hopefulness is imagining being powerful and rich. Other expressions of hope were witty and humourous, sometimes they were dark or bizarrely surreal, sometimes playful or ironic, sometimes in your face and confronting. These aspects surfaced particularly in the sketches and in the imaginative exercises when the young people were asked to imagine an image of hope that could be displayed in a museum exhibition. One young man came up with the following: 'Yoda's wearing a jet pack. He's got a chop stick in one hand and tries to steal food from visitors. He has a light sabre in the other hand. In this exhibit Yoda exists in a time when there is no food. There is a sign next to Yoda that that says "I'm hungry"'.

The Yoda image clearly suggests the importance of figures from popular culture in creating images of hope. There were numerous such popular culture figures in the images produced by the young people. Yoda is presented here as a trickster and as a warrior. His mission is to steal food, perhaps to feed the imagination of hope? Another young man came up with this scenario: 'there's a fish tank with a fish inside it. Next to the fish is a garden gnome who is smoking a pipe. Next to the gnome is the sign 'gone fishing' and the fish is saying "I'm not stupid". The gnome gets up into the fish tank and catches the fish and eats it'. In a sense hope can be absurd, sometimes even surreal. Such images seem to be significant in envisaging hope or just helping to provide or ignite a spark that can re-animate the imagination and the world.

The torn fabric and a difficult hope

Hopefulness can be difficult when experienced from a relatively poor situation, poor not in human affection, intelligence, creativity and so on, but poor in the material and educational resources required to attain the promises or even expectations our society creates of the good life. While the goals of hope may be similar for the marginalised and those in the mainstream, there are differences in the experiences of that hope, in its sense of distance and of being at a far remove, in the difficulty of attaining mobility, both imaginative and practical, towards realising it, in the probability of a long struggle to achieve it. Such hope can be clear and determined but also wounded, tentative and fragile.

O'Neill suggested that research of the kind we were undertaking should be 'governed by a profound respect for the particulars of place, time and conduct' (1975: 53). He stressed 'the ritual wholeness of the daily particulars which constitute the fabric of individual integrity and communal endurance. Every individual and community stands to us as a monument of human possibility expressed in the faces, the hands, the music, the food, dwellings and tools ... The cycle of these things is born in an expansion of hope and possibility' (1975: 52).

There is an infinite number of starting points and pathways that can lead to hope. The material in this book begins to map the richly complex and often tentative expressions of everyday hope. The look of hope and the imagination of hope begin to emerge. Not only do we see representations of hope, but also entry points for pathways leading towards hope, plus images of lived experiences and struggles for hope.

A journey both in and towards hope is an intimately imaginative one. Hope can revitalise imagination. Just the experience of hopefulness has value in its own right. These young people revealed the diversity of hopefulness and the modes by which hope can be imagined. They expressed hope as an inspiration or an aspiration; a radical shift in perspective that sometimes involved a breakthrough or at least a going beyond mundane limits; having a special place that was sometimes secret and outside everyday life; having family and friends whom you care for and who are the people who care for you and make you feel hopeful; being able do the normal things that you want to do; a return to better times; a result of provocation and risk; the ordinary made somehow different.

Hope can be a window through which a horizon becomes visible. It is a reminder that something important, a critical other dimension, has been lost or forgotten, even if we are unsure what exactly it is. Hope can be thought of as an openness to possibilities (Barcan 2002: 347). Hope is not necessarily future oriented in the literal sense of linear time, but it can offer access to a different order of experience and time, to a vertical dimension, a depth and source of imaginative life. Images of hope can be understood as 'healing fictions' (Hillman 1983). While the imagination shows us that things can be different, hopefulness suggests that change is still possible. It is a glimpse of, and faith in, something better.

Hope can simply be an urge towards some ideal, or a refusal to accept the conditions of the present. As well as a kind of shining light at the end of the tunnel, a glimmer on the horizon, hope may have its origins in the words 'hopping' or 'jumping'. Hope is here imagined as a 'leap, with expectation' (Partridge 1966: 295). Audacious or even surreal imaginative leaps can produce unexpected associations and land us in places that no amount of clear logic or realism could possibly reach: 'there are five green creatures that aren't human. They are about human size, with weird faces. The creatures are talking to each in other in their own language. They're friendly'. Friendly aliens suggest that an intimation of hope can be something that originates from outside the normal ecology of everyday expectations. In this sense, hope can seem to come from somewhere else.

The hope of things

While we may dream of grand projects, we are reminded by John O'Neill that 'things beckon us back—the weight of things, their touch, their smell; the time of things, their seasons; the way of things, their uses—all these offer us a chance of salvation, a redemption rooted in things' (1975: 10). Images of things—tools, buildings, cars, buses, feet—can be found throughout this book, both in the photographs and the fantasies. Things are commonly presented as a crucial resource in contemporary society's vision of the good life and in how to attain it. In just about every society ever known, things have been used to mark identity and relationship, to beautify or stigmatise, to express something about the person who made it, acquired it or gave it as a gift. Things bring strength, power and often membership. But in contemporary consumer capitalism, this practice has become hyper-dimensional and acquired a whole new set of inflections.

Glossy and provocative images of consumption are constantly paraded before us, but 'many people do not have the same opportunity to share in the bounty of society, nor do they have the same opportunity to contest the meaning of things. The meaning of these cultural objects is not given, nor is it fixed' (Ozanne et al. 1998: 185). Interestingly, there are no images in this book of famous brands, no images of shopping malls or other palaces of consumption. The things presented by the young people are far more personal and idiosyncratic. There is a difference perhaps between hope for something and something that generates hope. These things may have once been commodities but are now relocated in slightly different contexts, and new meanings have evolved. The Yoda image discussed earlier scarcely functions as a literal role model or as an emissary of rampant consumerism or as an inspiration for corporate allegiance.

Ortega Y Gasset suggested that 'things do not interest us because they do not find in us favourable surfaces on which to be reflected, and it is necessary for us to multiply the facets of our mind so that an infinite number of themes may penetrate it (1963: 35). So the things presented here as objects of hope challenge us to see ordinary things in extraordinary ways. 'Everything has within it an indication of its possible plenitude', insisted Y Gasset (1963: 32). The camera work by the young people brings a different perspective to things, a different filter of the world. It reveals challenging images with 'multiple meanings' (Cook & Hess 2007: 43) that are important in communicating ideas both to themselves and to adults.

In his *Odes Elementales*, Pablo Neruda celebrated the poetics of ordinary objects (1972), while Rilke praised the loyalty of small, everyday habits and things in our lives, things that come to our aid when we need them, that repay our care of them (1967). Y Gasset put it bluntly: 'The fact is that when we have reached the depths of pessimism and do not seem to find anything positive enough in the universe to save us, our eyes turn towards the small things of daily living ... We see, then, that it is not the great things, the great pleasures, nor the great ambitions which keep us alive upon the face of the earth ...' (1963: 47). Hope can reanimate everyday things and help us gain another, more vibrant or curiously different perspective on an otherwise mundane, entrapping, going-nowhere everydayness. Hope can show that there is symbolic depth and psychological complexity at the very heart of apparently mundane things, the everyday world of flatland. From this perspective, hopefulness comes, not from elsewhere or outside, but from a heightened sense of the familiar. Sharing this with friends is good because it means you aren't alone. Sharing the play and pleasure of this reality-shifting builds relationships.

A place for hope

There is a geography of hope. Sometimes it contains safe and familiar places—a teenaged girl's bedroom, the backyard of the family home, a beach, a city street. At other times the places can be those of fantasy and reverie—magical, mysterious, hidden (Bachelard 1994): 'there's a garden with large trees, grass, dappled light and flowers. The garden smells clean'. The garden is reached by a long hard walk where the walker moves away from civilisation. It's a secret garden, it's a silent place, without people, a garden located in the future.

Hopefulness can be evoked when we enter another space and time. Hope doesn't only come from looking into the future, but also with the past, indeed any time other than this one we inhabit now. The important point is that there is another time to this one, another place, another experience that is available. Hopefulness can be about getting back something that you thought was gone, of finding a pathway back. One of the young men took some photos of an abandoned primary school that he had attended. It was a place that was once important to him. Perhaps unexpectedly, he remarked that he had enjoyed primary school, so this was a site which gave him memories of pleasure and happiness.

It suggests that hopefulness can come from remembering a place—real or imagined—in the past, where one's life, one's future, felt good, and where one had a sense of possibilities. Hope comes from being able to return to such a place. Not always an easy journey. This place and time are markers beyond which life took a wrong pathway. They are resources for re-imagining a different, better turn of events, for remembering a better feeling about oneself and ones relationship to and with the world. Such a marker can help reactivate a movement into this better life. In this case the site is a public place, yet also an intimate one. It is a site of respect and achievement, plus often one of rebellion and protest. It is part of mainstream ordinary kids' lives: school.

Framing hope

I have suggested that handling hope, especially the difficult, everyday hope presented by these young people, with its ambivalence and contradictions, its often mundaneness and its fleeting fragility in a context of frustration and marginalisation, is a work that requires patience. The work should move indirectly, gathering images. It should be circular rather than linear, what Y Gasset termed 'wide circles of attention' (1963: 53). Our presentation of these hopeful images needs to allow for resonance between the images and between them and broader associations. There need to be constructive spaces of doubt. We need to be careful not to over interpret, nor to strain in order to find significance in every detail.

Part of the work involves trying to find an appropriate vocabulary for hope, one that sustains the sense of imaginative play and does justice to the emotional investment and to any humour that is present. A trust and confidence in working with fantasy images rather than simply interrogating, is essential. As Judith Brown wrote, 'Our desires, dreams, and longings, are given their form by the imagination; they are how hope is cast by the imagination' (2003: 2).

references

Bachelard G (1988) *Air and dreams: An essay on the imagination of movement,* E Farrell & C Farrell (trans.). Dallas: Dallas Institute Publications (original work published 1943).

Bachelard G (1994) *The poetics of space,* M Jolas (trans.). Boston: Bacon Press (original work published 1958).

Beck U (1992) *Risk society: towards a new modernity.* London: Sage.

Barcan R (2002) 'Problems without Solutions: teaching theory and the politics of hope', *Continuum: Journal of Media & Cultural Studies,* 16 (3): 344–56.

Brown J (2003) 'Ernst Bloch and the Utopian Imagination', *Eras Journal,* 2003.

Bloch E & Adorno T (1988) 'Something's missing: a discussion between Ernst Bloch and Theodor W Adorno on the contradictions of utopian longing', in E Bloch, *The utopian function of art and literature: selected essays,* J Zipes & F Mecklenburg (trans.). London and Cambridge, Mass.: MIT Press (original work published 1964).

Braithwaite J (2004) 'Emancipation and Hope', *Annals of the American Academy of Political and Social Science,* 592: 79–98.

Braithwaite V (2004a) 'Preface: Collective Hope', *Annals of the American Academy of Political and Social Science,* 592, 6–15.

Burnett J (2004) 'Community, Cohesion and the State', *Race & Class,* 45 (3): 1–18.

Clay G (1989) 'Ephemeral Places', *Design Quarterly,* 143: 1–35.

Cook T & Hess E (2007) 'What the Camera Sees and From Whose Perspective: Fun Methodologies for engaging children in enlightening adults', *Childhood,* 14 (1): 29–45.

Connell RW (2000) *The Men and the Boys.* Sydney: Allen & Unwin.

Cornell D (2005) 'The Gift of the Future', *Differences: A journal of Feminist Cultural Studies,* 16 (3): 68–75.

Derrida, J (1992) *Deconstruction and the Possibility of Justice,* Cornell, Carlson & Rosenfeld (eds). New York: Routledge.

Derrida J (1994) *Specters of Marx: the state of the debt, the work of mourning, and the new international,* P Kamuf (trans.). New York: Routledge.

Eheart BK, Hopping D, Power MB, Mitchell ET & Racine D (2009) 'Generations of Hope Communities: An intergenerational neighbourhood model of support and service', *Children and Youth Services Review,* 31: 47–52.

Friere P (1994) *Pedagogy of hope: Reliving Pedagogy of the Oppressed.* London: Continuum.

Halpin D (2003) 'Hope, utopianism and educational renewal', the encyclopaedia of informal education <www.infed.org/biblio/hope.htm>.

Hillman J (1983) *Healing Fiction.* Station Hill: Barrytown.

hooks b (1994) *Teaching to transgress: Education as the practice of freedom.* New York: Routledge.

Johansson T (2000) 'Moral panics revisited', *Young,* 8 (1): 22–35.

Kraftl P (2005) 'Ruining utopia', *Skandalon,* 1 (1).

McGeer V (2004) 'The Art of Good Hope', *Annals of the American Academy of Political and Social Science,* 592 (1): 100–127.

Marinetti FT (1914) 'Geometric and mechanical splendor and the numerical sensibility'.

Mistral WR & Evans S (2002) 'An Innovative Project for Young People in Care Who have been Sexually Abused', *British Journal of Social Work,* 32: 321–33.

More T (1516) *Utopia.*

Nancy J-L (1991) *The inoperative community,* P Connor (ed.), Connor, Garbus, Holland and Sawhney (trans.). Minneapolis: University of Minnesota Press.

Neruda P (1972) *Selected Poems.* New York: Delta.

O'Neill J (1975) *Making Sense Together.* New York: Harper and Row.

Oakeshott M (1962) *Rationalism in Politics and Other Essays,* London: Methuen &Co.

Ozanne J, Hill R & Wright N (1998) 'Juvenile Delinquent's Use of Consumption as Cultural Resistance: implications for Juvenile Reform Programs and Public Policy', *Journal of Public Policy and Marketing,* 17 (2): 185–96.

Partridge E (1966) *Origins.* London: Routledge & Kegan Paul.

Piper C (2001) 'Who are these Youths? Language in the Service of Policy', *Youth Justice,* 1 (2): 30–9.

Raaijmakers QAW, Engels CME & Van Hoof A (2005) 'Delinquency and moral reasoning in adolescence and young adulthood', *International Journal of Behavorial Development,* 29 (3): 247–58.

Rilke M (1967) *Duino Elegies.* New York: W. W. Norton.

Royale N (2003) *The uncanny.* New York: Routledge.

SACE Board of SA. New SACE information,<www.saceboard.sa.edu.au/newsace/faq.htm>

Sennett R (2003) *Respect: the formation of character in a world of inequality.* London and New York: Allan Lane.

Shearing C & Kempa M (2004) 'A Museum of Hope: A Story of Robben Island', *Annals of the American Academy of Political and Social Science,* 592: 62–78.

Smith J (2007) 'Ye've got to 'ave balls to play this game sir! Boys, peers and fears: The negative influence of school-based "cultural accomplices" in constructing hegemonic masculinities', *Gender and Education,* 19 (2): 179–98.

Synder CR (2002) 'Hope Theory: Rainbows in the Mind', *Psychological Inquiry,* 13 (4): 249–75.

Welch M, Price EA & Yankey N (2002) 'Moral Panic Over Youth Violence: Wilding and the Manufacture of Menace in the Media', *Youth Society,* 34 (3): 3–30.

White M & Epston M (1990) *Narrative means to therapeutic ends.* New York: Norton.

Y Gasset O (1963) *Meditations on Quixote.* New York: WW Norton.

Zembylas M (2005) *Teaching with emotion: A Postmodern Enactment.* Greenwich, Connecticut: Information Age Publishing.